The Bu
Guide to
Walt Disney World 2016

By Jeffrey Merola

ISBN #978-0692642795

The Busy Family's Guide to Walt Disney World 2016 / Jeffrey Merola

website = www.mousevacationplanning.com
email = jmerola@mousevacationplanning.com
twitter = @JMerolaWDW
facebook = facebook.com/pages/mouse-vacation-planning

This book is dedicated to my wife, Lori, and my children who were always there for me and supported me in every way possible. We have made many special memories together when we have visited Walt Disney World. The book is also dedicated to my dad and mom, Merino & JoAnne, who always taught me to never give up.

Table of Contents

Introduction

Who am I, and why am I writing this guide to Walt Disney World?

My name is Jeffrey Merola. I am a husband and a father of a fourteen year old daughter and a ten year old son. In addition, I am an author, a New York State elementary teacher of seventeen years and have also coached high school football for twenty-two years. In addition, I have been an Authorized Disney Vacation Planner for the past three years.

Back in 1977, when I was five years old, my family went on a vacation to Walt Disney World. Unfortunately, the only part of the trip I remember was the attraction “It's a Small World.”

Twenty years went by and I had no desire to return to Walt Disney World. Then, in the summer of 1997, my almost fiancée, Lori, came to me and asked if I wanted to go to Walt Disney World during our February break. At first, I was against the idea, figuring the trip would be a huge waste of time and money. Why would the two of us want to vacation with what seemed like a million kids when we already work in an elementary school? However, Lori convinced me it was a good idea. So, I pulled out my credit card, we boarded a plane, and I tried to put a smile on my face. Honestly, I wasn't expecting much. However, I was very wrong.

We had an incredible time. We stayed at Disney's All Star Sports Resort and went to the theme parks from morning until night every day. We were exhausted, but had smiles from ear to ear. Ultimately, my greatest disappointment was when we had to return to reality.

Since that trip, I have visited the home of the "Mouse" approximately 220 fun filled days. I consider Walt Disney World my second home. I primarily vacation there during winter break, which is in February (President's Day week for us New Yorkers), but I have also visited during spring break, November, December, May, and a number of times during the summer. I even decided to take a two day trip to get engaged on Walt Disney World property. The last few years I have visited three to four times a year to continually research for my books. I obviously have become a huge Walt Disney World fan.

Those Walt Disney World vacations have helped me build many wonderful memories. One of the best was when my wife and I took our daughter, Megan, for the first time in February 2003. She was only sixteen months old, but we wanted her to experience Walt Disney World at an early age. Our parents thought we were crazy to bring a child that young. But, we ignored their advice, packed our clothes, got the diaper bag together, and jumped in the family truckster (i.e. our van).

The first theme park we took Megan to was Disney's MGM Studios, which is now named Disney's Hollywood Studios. It was the first park to open that morning, and I was anxious for her to meet the "Mouse." When Megan got into the park, I turned to look at my wife and she had tears of joy in her eyes.

It really touched me beyond anything I could imagine to see how much this meant to Lori, who always wanted to go as a little girl, but never did. She was now fulfilling that dream through her daughter's eyes.

We all had an amazing time that year and Megan loved it all! She even clapped and cheered while watching Beauty and the Beast Live on Stage.

In February of 2006, my family and I again traveled to see the "Mouse." This time my wife and I had my eight month old son, Merino, my mother, JoAnne, my daughter, and my mother-in-law, Linda, along with us for all the Disney magic. My mother had not been to Walt Disney World since the trip we went on in 1977, 29 years earlier.

We entered out first theme park that year, the Magic Kingdom, and strolled down Main Street, U.S.A, admiring Cinderella's Castle in the distance. By the time we had made it to our character breakfast at Crystal Palace, my mom had gotten misty eyes. She wiped some tears of joy, turned on a huge smile, and gave us all a kiss.

Eight years ago, I began to write about what I have learned and knew about Walt Disney World through all of my visits. I began to walk through the theme parks with a critical eye but was hard pressed to find any flaws. I believe it is truly a magical place! My family and I were continually entertained and enjoyed incredible sights and sounds throughout the theme parks. We have been able to taste incredible food in the Walt Disney World restaurants, and being 100% Italian, I have thoroughly enjoyed that aspect as well!

This book is my 7th Walt Disney World book and the 5th in the series of Busy Family Guides. Every year I work on improving the book to make it the best possible for my readers. I am very excited about this 2016 edition with all the improvements and additions.

My book will assist your busy family plan a memorable trip to Walt Disney World and get you through the theme parks stress free! I know all too well that busy families do not have time to read a six hundred page book to go on vacation. So, I have written a more concise Walt Disney World guide book that will help the busy family plan their vacation and assist them with everything in Walt Disney World. The book will go in-depth about Walt Disney World and it will give you all my tips to have a memorable and magical vacation!

Chapter 1 - Walt Disney World (WDW)

Walt Disney World is an incredible resort complex that is located in Lake Buena Vista, Florida. Lake Buena Vista is a suburb of Orlando, Florida. Disney refers to all visitors in their theme parks as guests and the 60,000 plus workers they employ as cast members. WDW is 47 square miles in size and it is made up of four theme parks (Magic Kingdom, Epcot, Disney's Hollywood Studios, and Disney's Animal Kingdom), two water parks (Blizzard Beach and Typhoon Lagoon), Disney Springs which was formerly Downtown Disney (shopping), Disney's Wide World of Sports Complex, Disney Quest (will close in 2016 and the NBA Experience will replace it), four Championship Golf Courses, two miniature golf courses, and 25 resorts.

The Magic Kingdom was the first theme park built in Walt Disney World. It is home to one of the most recognizable structures on the planet, Cinderella's Castle. There are seven separate sections or lands in the Magic Kingdom. They are: Main Street, USA, Tomorrowland, Liberty Square, Frontierland, Adventureland, Storybook Circus, and Fantasyland. All sections contain rides and shows, which Disney refers to as attractions, and restaurants.

Magic Kingdom

EPCOT was the second theme park built in WDW. The initials in EPCOT stand for Experimental Prototype Community Of Tomorrow. Walt Disney himself created the name and the concept for the park long before it was built. It is made up of Future World and World Showcase. Future World has technology, thrill attractions, and restaurants. World Showcase is made up of 11 different countries that contain attractions and restaurants. The icon in EPCOT is Spaceship Earth which houses a ride for guests to enjoy.

Disney's Hollywood Studios was the third theme park built in WDW. The theme park is based on various Hollywood movies. The Disney Studios has several different types of attractions and restaurants. The attractions in the park are based on more than just Disney movies. It is especially known for its fabulous thrill rides, including the Tower of Terror and the Rock 'n' Roller Coaster Starring Aerosmith.

Disney's Animal Kingdom was the fourth theme park built in Walt Disney World. Many people assume this theme park is similar to a zoo. However, so much more is incorporated into this theme park. Animal Kingdom does have several live animals to see while on a walking tour or a safari jeep tour. This may be surprising to some guests, but the animals are in their natural habitat and not in cages. The theme park also has many attractions that revolve around the animal theme. The theme park's icon is the Tree of Life.

The two water parks in WDW are Blizzard Beach and Typhoon Lagoon. Blizzard Beach is a ski resort that is melting in the hot Florida sun. The theme of Typhoon Lagoon is around a tropical island. Both water parks are fabulous and have numerous wonderful attractions.

Disney Springs is comprised of numerous shops and restaurants. You can purchase almost anything you can think of with Disney's name on it in the shopping area.

Disney's Wide World of Sports Complex hosts many sports teams for tournaments and events from around the world. The complex also hosts numerous running events. A schedule can be found at rundisney.com.

Recreation is a part of WDW too. You can golf on one of four championship courses, play miniature golf on two different courses, play volleyball, rent a boat, fish, and all types of other activities. You can reserve a tee time at the Palm, Magnolia, Lake Buena Vista, or Oak Trail golf course by calling (407) WDW-GOLF.

Walt Disney World has a special area for little girls who want to feel like a princess. The Bibbidi Bobbidi Boutique will transform your little girl into a bona fide Disney Princess of their choosing. It is located in the Magic Kingdom in Cinderella's Castle right across from Cinderella's Royal Table and in Disney Springs.

Your little girl can have her hair done, make up applied, receive a Princess sash, and/or nails manicured. You do need to make reservations for this service and pricing starts at around $55 and can go up to $250, which would include a princess dress.

There is now a new Disney Frozen package available for children ages 3-12 in the Bibbidi Bobbidi Boutique. Your child can choose to have either Anna hairstyling with or without the costume or Elsa hairstyling with or without the costume. They will receive make up, nails manicured, a Princess sash, a Princess cinch bag, and a 12 inch Olaf stuffed animal. Call (407) WDW-7895 to make a reservation.

Walt Disney World has a special area for boys, girls, and grown – ups who want to be transformed into a pirate. It is called the Pirates League and it is located in the Magic Kingdom in Adventureland. The guest wishing to be a pirate will be transformed using a facial effect, bandanna, eye patch, and many other pirate accessories. The cost of the Pirates League begins at $29.95 and up to $75 plus tax and reservations are highly recommended. The number to call is (407) WDW – CREW. The reservation times are between 9am and 4pm.

Chapter 2 - Walt Disney World Resorts

There are three different categories of resorts segmented by price in WDW. The first are obviously identified as the **value** resorts. They are the lowest in price. Currently there are five: Disney's All Star Movies Resort, Disney's All Star Music Resort, Disney's All Star Sports Resort, Disney's Pop Century Resort, and Disney's newest value resort is Disney's Art of Animation Resort. Each of these resorts range in price from approximately $85 to $175 plus tax per night for a standard room, depending upon the time of year you are visiting Walt Disney World. A preferred room will add approximately $20 per night.

The second set of resorts are identified as **moderate** and are approximately $70 more per night than the value resorts. These include: Disney's Caribbean Beach Resort, Disney's Coronado Springs, Disney's Port Orleans French Quarter, and Disney's Port Orleans Riverside. Depending on availability, they will cost approximately $165 to $255 plus tax per night for a standard room, depending upon the time of year you are visiting Walt Disney World. A preferred or water view room can add up to $60 per night.

The third and final are **deluxe / vacation club** resorts. They are: Disney's Animal Kingdom Lodge, Disney's Animal Kingdom Villas, Disney's Bay Lake Tower, Disney's Beach Club, Disney's Beach Club Villas, Disney's Boardwalk Inn, Disney's

Boardwalk Villas, Disney's Contemporary Resort, Walt Disney World Dolphin, Disney's Grand Floridian Resort & Spa, Disney's Old Key West Resort, Disney's Polynesian Village, Disney's Polynesian Villas and Bungalows, Disney's Saratoga Springs Resort & Spa, Disney's Tree House Villas, Walt Disney World Swan, Disney's Wilderness Lodge, The Villas at Disney's Grand Floridian Resort & Spa, The Villas at Disney's Wilderness Lodge, and Disney's Yacht Club Resort. They range in price from $285 to $760 plus tax per night for a standard room. Please note that the Swan and Dolphin are not operated by Walt Disney World. They are only on Walt Disney World property.

One other resort caters to the outdoor adventurer guest. Disney's Fort Wilderness and Campground has a campground theme and is priced for as low as $50 per night to $135 for campsites and $295 to $465 for the wilderness cabins.

Disney's Fort Wilderness

Now that you have the information on the resort names, you need to decide which one is the best for your family and your budget. Make that decision as early as possible. I would encourage you to make this decision eight months or more in advance to ensure you get the resort of your choice.

There are many other factors that can help you decide which resort is best for you. Most standard rooms in WDW sleep four and a child under three in a portable crib. Most of the deluxe resorts do sleep five and a few moderate resorts now sleep five as well.

The All Star Resorts are very busy, large, and crowded. They typically have groups and sports teams staying there because Walt Disney World hosts many tournaments for baseball, basketball, cheerleading, lacrosse, soccer, and softball. The All Star Resorts do share buses with each other when traveling to certain theme parks. One other drawback is that the resorts do not have a slide in their pool area. However, the All Star Resorts are a perfect fit for a family on a budget.

My wife and I stayed at the All Star Sports for many years and had a blast. It was busy, but we were not in the resort that often. When my children were young we again stayed at the All Star Sports. The room was an average sized hotel room and the food court was just what we needed while the children were little.

Disney's All Star Sports Resort

Disney's Port Orleans French Quarter is a spectacular family resort and it is not overwhelming. We stayed there for a number of years. The hotel room was slightly larger than a value resort room and the resort was very quiet. However, the rooms do only accommodate four guests and a child under three in a porta crib that is provided. You can choose to stay in a room that has a standard view, garden view, pool view, or river view. Your view choice can increase the price per night.

Disney's Port Orleans French Quarter

Disney's Caribbean Beach Resort is beautiful, but very large. The resort has five separate bus pick up locations to bring guests to the theme parks because of the resort's size. However, most of the rooms now accommodate five people. You can choose from a room with a standard view, water or pool view. You can choose to stay in a pirate room or a preferred room as well which would be closest to the main building.

Disney's Caribbean Beach Resort

Disney's Port Orleans Riverside is a large resort with four different bus pick up locations to take you to the theme parks. The resort can accommodate a family of five in a standard room as well. Some different room view choices include: standard, pool, river, and garden. You can choose a preferred room too which would place you closer to the main building.

If you are a family of six and on a budget, then WDW has family suites in the All Star Music and Art of Animation Resorts. They range in price from $210 to $460 plus tax per night, depending upon the time of year you are visiting WDW.

The deluxe resorts have suites within the resorts that are considerably more expensive. For example, you could pay as high as $3,600 per night in Disney's Grand Floridian Resort & Spa in the Main Building Club Level Grand Suite. You could also pay $1,100 per night in a 1 bedroom suite in the Contemporary Resort. These are only two examples, but you can see the wide range of prices that exists. It definitely all depends on what your budget is for your vacation.

If your family wants to stay in either a moderate or deluxe resort, but can't decide, there are a few items to consider. If you have the money to spend, then opt for the deluxe resort. They all have unique themes and outstanding service. However, if you want to save some money, then stick with a moderate resort. Moderate resorts have slides for their pool areas, just like the deluxe resorts. They are typically half the price of a deluxe resort and still provide you with the outstanding Disney themes and service. Remember, on a Walt Disney World vacation, you are seldom in your room. You are usually out and about in Walt Disney World!

All of the Walt Disney World resorts are excellent, but I have my favorites. The ones I would recommend from each category are:

- **Disney's Port Orleans French Quarter (moderate):** The resort is possibly the smallest in Walt Disney World and is themed after New Orleans. It has a great food court that is small, quiet, and manageable. I highly recommend trying the beignets. This New Orleans favorite is fried dough with a powdered sugar topping. There is even boat transportation in the back of the resort to Disney Springs which was named Downtown Disney.

Disney's Port Orleans French Quarter

- **Disney's Beach Club (deluxe):** The resort is gorgeous and has the best and most unique pool area I have ever seen, including a sandy bottom and a lazy river. The resort is home to my favorite restaurant in the world, Cape May. The resort has numerous room choices that include standard rooms, pool and garden views, and even suites. You can walk out the back doors of the resort and be on the Boardwalk, which is similar to boardwalks in New Jersey and Maryland. You can take a 5 minute walk over to Epcot or Disney's Hollywood Studios from the Boardwalk.

Disney's Beach Club Resort

- **Disney's Contemporary Resort (deluxe):** The Contemporary is one of the original resorts and it is on the monorail loop. The monorail travels through the resort and it will take you on your journey to the Magic Kingdom. You and your family can also choose to walk to the Magic Kingdom on a walking trail too. Chef Mickey's is located within the magical walls of the Contemporary. You can choose a view of the Magic Kingdom from your room which will be more expensive than a standard view room.

Disney's Contemporary Resort

- **Disney's Bay Lake Tower (deluxe):** The resort has a futuristic theme and is incredibly quiet. It contains deluxe studios, 1 bedroom suites, and 2 bedroom suites. Families have the luxury of walking over to the Magic Kingdom from the resort. Families have the option of viewing the Magic Kingdom fireworks, named Wishes, from the top of the resort, while listening to the "Wishes" music.

Bay Lake Tower

- **Disney's All Star Sports Resort (value):** The resort buildings are identified by sport themes such as: football (touchdown), baseball, basketball, and tennis. It even has a football field that families can play on and larger than life sports icons and equipment. There are only two types of rooms. They are standard rooms or preferred rooms which are closer to the food court. The food court is enormous and has multiple food choices for breakfast, lunch, and dinner.

Disney's All Star Sports Resort

- **Disney's Pop Century (value):** Families can journey back to the 50s, 60s, 70s, 80s, and 90s in this resort. It has giant sized memorabilia from the different decades and the food court is family friendly with numerous choices for everyone. There is even a walkway in the back of the resort over to Disney's Art of Animation Resort.

Disney's Pop Century Resort

- **Disney's Grand Floridian Resort and Spa (deluxe):** The resort is absolutely gorgeous and breathtaking. It is a five star resort and is home to a world class spa. It has six restaurants. They range from being upscale to quick service establishments. One of my family's favorites is 1900 Park Fare. You even have the option to view the Magic Kingdom from your room, but this option does come with an additional cost.

Disney's Grand Floridian Resort & Spa

- **Disney's Art of Animation Resort (value):** The resort is the newest value resort in Walt Disney World. The grounds are like stepping into a Disney movie. The resort contains a large food court for breakfast, lunch, and dinner. The feature pool is the largest pool of any resort on property. There are two different types of room choices. The resort contains Little Mermaid standard rooms which sleep four and a child under three in a pack-n-play. The resort has family suites that sleep six as well. They are: Cars family suites, Finding Nemo family suites, Lion King family suites, and family suites that are not based after any Disney movie. Please note that if Disney is offering a discount of any kind the discount will usually work for some of the family suites, but the Little Mermaid rooms are never discounted.

Disney's Art of Animation Resort

- **Disney's Polynesian Village Resort (deluxe):** When you walk into the Polynesian it is like taking a step into Hawaii. It is a spectacular resort and you will be greeted with an "Aloha!" from courteous and friendly cast members. The resort is home to the restaurant 'Ohana, where you can eat breakfast with Mickey. Your family will be very close to the Magic Kingdom since it is on the monorail loop. Since you are so close to the Magic Kingdom you do have the option of staying in a room with a theme park view!

Disney's Polynesian Village Resort

- **Disney's Animal Kingdom Lodge (deluxe):** This deluxe resort is spectacular like all the others, but it includes its own special niche. The resort is located near Disney's Animal Kingdom theme park so you are able to view the animals walking in the savannah in certain areas of the resort. All rooms do not have a view of the savannah, but there are some where you can see giraffes and many other beautiful animals right from your balcony. The resort is home to a few delicious restaurants, including a family favorite of ours called Boma.

Disney's Animal Kingdom Lodge

Disney's Animal Kingdom Lodge

Chapter 3

Should you stay in a Walt Disney World resort or stay off site? (Chapter includes information on Disney's Magical Express and extra magic hours)

My opinion is to absolutely stay in a Walt Disney World resort **100%** of the time. This is especially true during one of the school breaks. There are numerous perks that you will receive by staying at a Walt Disney World resort that you would otherwise not receive if you stayed off site. These perks are as follows:

1) All guests staying at a Walt Disney World resort receive complimentary shuttle and luggage service from Orlando International Airport to their resort upon arrival, then back to the airport when guests check out. This service is called **Disney's Magical Express Service.**

Disney's Magical Express sign

A few weeks before your trip, Disney will send you an envelope with your flight information and yellow luggage tags. Place the tags on your luggage handles of the bags you are checking in at the airport so Disney knows what bags to pick up for you. After your plane arrives at Orlando International Airport secure your MagicBand **(these will be explained very soon)** on your wrist and you can proceed directly to the Disney's Magical Express Service area. You will by-pass baggage claim. Disney's Magical Express is in the main terminal building, B side, level 1.

When you arrive a Disney cast member will scan your MagicBand. You and your family will board a Disney's Magical Express shuttle, and your luggage will show up in your resort room. Make sure to bring a change of clothes, pjs, and toiletries in your carry-on bag just in case the luggage gets to your resort room late.

Disney's Magical Express bus

This service must be set up with Disney approximately eight weeks before your trip or earlier. Please note, if your plane arrives after 10pm, you will have to get your own checked bags and then go to the Magical Express area. The easiest way to set up Disney's Magical Express is to call 1-866-599-0951.

2) You do not have to rent a car. Walt Disney World has an entire fleet of transportation waiting for you from buses to boats to monorails. Disney will take you anywhere within Walt Disney World. You can travel from your resort to all four theme parks, Disney Springs, and the water parks.

The one piece of information you do need to know is that the buses do not go from resort to resort. If you were planning on eating at a resort different from your own, you would have to travel to a theme park or Disney Springs first, and then take a bus from there to the other resort.

If you drive to Walt Disney World, and don't plan to use their transportation, you still have the benefit of being a Disney resort guest and will not have to pay for parking anywhere on Disney property. However, if you are not a Walt Disney World resort guest, then you will have to pay $20 a day to park at any of the theme parks.

3) You and your family remain enclosed within the Disney magic the entire time you are on your vacation. No one creates themes like Disney, and their cast members are superb at customer service. They go above and beyond to make you feel

right at home, and ensure that you have a magical experience.

4) You can take advantage of Disney's extra magic hours. These are extra hours in the theme parks that are only available to Walt Disney World resort guests. Disney usually will have a theme park open one hour early on a particular day and another theme park may stay open late two extra hours after the official closing time. During these precious hours, only Disney resort guests will be able to enjoy the magical attractions. There is no extra charge to take advantage of these hours. The extra magic hours are especially helpful during the school break times of February (President's Day week), holiday breaks, and spring break in March or April, since attendance is extremely high during these times.

5) You have the luxury of returning to your resort and take a break in the afternoon, and then return to a theme park at dinner time. All you need to do is board your resort bus, and it will take you back to your resort.

If you stay off WDW property, you will have to drive off property, which will take longer, or wait for a hotel shuttle that actually only comes a few times during the day. Whereas, the Walt Disney World buses run every 15 to 20 minutes.

6) If you buy a souvenir at one of the theme parks or Disney Springs, you do not have to carry it with you all day. You can ask the cast member to have it sent back to your resort at no charge to you.

7) Walt Disney World resort guests can now participate in MyMagic+. MyMagic+ is an experience that Disney has officially in place. After you book your vacation, you will then visit the website **mydisneyexperience.com.** You will create a free account at this website. Through the website you will be able to customize your own MagicBands. The MagicBands have replaced the Key to the World card that Disney used for years. The MagicBand will act as your resort room key, theme park ticket, charge card, dining plan, Magical Express reservation, and FastPass+ ticket.

FastPass+ is available for most attractions. By obtaining a FastPass+ reservation, you are reserving a time for the given attraction with little to no wait. You can sign up online for FastPass+ before your vacation. You can sign up for three FastPass+ attractions for one park per day 60 days in advance. However, if you are staying off WDW property and you have your Magic Your Way tickets in hand (theme park admission tickets), you can sign up for three FastPass+ attractions per day only 30 days in advance. **Please refer to Chapter Six for a detailed description of FastPass+.**

FastPass+ also offers you the opportunity to select shows, character meet and greets, parade viewing locations, and firework viewing locations.

The MagicBands can be used for saving photos that are taken by Disney photographers and the photos taken while you are on certain attractions. This service is called Memory Maker which replaces the Photo Pass. The service does cost $149 if you purchase it ahead of time, and $169 if you purchase it after you arrive in Walt Disney World.

8) As a Walt Disney World Resort guest, you have the option of purchasing one of the dining plans. These can be very cost effective and give you the opportunity to eat at many restaurants that you may not have chosen to visit for a meal. People staying off property cannot purchase a dining plan. I will go into more detail about the dining plan later in this book.

9) When you stay in a Walt Disney World resort, you are guaranteed admission into a Disney theme park even if the park is at capacity. You may think that this never happens. However, Christmas Day is typically one of the busiest days of the year, and the Magic Kingdom usually does fill to capacity. If this happens on Christmas Day or any other time, as a resort guest you cannot be turned away. You show a cast member your MagicBand, they will scan it, and they will let you through the gates. People staying off property will not be allowed to enter.

10) Some little perks of Walt Disney World resorts that I have always enjoyed is you can watch your own resort TV channel. The channel has constant updates of events around Walt Disney World, including park hours, and park favorites.

One additional perk is a personal family favorite of mine, the wakeup call. Mickey Mouse himself or a select Disney character will call you to get you up and going. If your children are like mine, they'll love hearing this voice first thing in the morning.

11) When your vacation sadly comes to an end, you can check in with your airline right at your Walt Disney World resort. Each resort provides you with the opportunity to secure your boarding passes and check your bags. This must be done the day of your return flight and at least four hours in advance of your departure. Your front desk staff can assist you in locating their resort's airline check in. The airline check - in desk is open from 5am - 1pm. Alaska, American, Delta, JetBlue, Southwest, and United all participate in this option.

People have told me they think it is beneficial to stay outside of Walt Disney World because of the price. I do agree that this is possible. However, my opinion is that the cost does not outweigh all the advantages you will benefit from if you are a Walt Disney World resort guest.

The hotels off property have many claims that are not entirely true. They will claim that they are just outside of Disney's front gate and they have shuttle service to Walt Disney World. This is true, but the off-site hotels do not tell you that Walt Disney World is 47 square miles. At peak times of the day, especially during rush hour, it may take as long as 30 minutes to an hour to just get to the parking lot of a theme park.

The off-site hotels do have shuttle services, but they don't tell you that the shuttles only run at certain times of the day. The Disney buses run every 15 to 20 minutes.

Stay at a Walt Disney World resort. It will maximize your vacation for your entire family, and it will be a magical experience!

Chapter 4

Planning your trip

(Information on Magic Your Way tickets, Disney dining plans, booking dining, and the Fantasmic dining package)

You've decided to visit the happiest place on Earth, Walt Disney World. However, the most important question has yet to be answered. When do you visit the "Mouse?"

If you have school age children, then you most likely will visit during one of the school breaks. Spring break is during March or April, depending upon where you live. Approximately four areas of the United States have a winter break. This occurs during President's week in February. The other school break is during every child's favorite time, the summer. Walt Disney World is considerably crowded during all of these times.

You may want to visit during Christmas, Easter, or Thanksgiving. These are the busiest times of the year in WDW and the most expensive. The benefit would definitely be experiencing the magic Disney brings during a holiday season. Walt Disney World is absolutely spectacular during the Christmas season with the decorations and holiday cheer throughout the "World."

Cinderella's Castle in December

Let's face it, WDW always has people in the theme parks. There are certain times of the year that are less chaotic than others. The months of September, early October, early December, January, early February, and early May are considerably less crowded than other times of the year.

Next, decide on the resort you are going to stay in. Make sure to refer back to chapter two to assist you with this decision. When you have decided on a resort, you need to call WDW travel (1-407-WDISNEY), visit disneyworld.com, or contact me directly. Along with being an author, I am an Authorized Disney Vacation Planner and Disney only travel agent. I own Mouse

Vacation Planning and I am affiliated with a sister travel company. My email is **jmerola@mousevacationplanning.com** and my website is www.mousevacationplanning.com. All the prices I have are through Disney because I work directly with them. I will make your vacation magical with a personal touch!

When you are speaking with a travel agent, always ask if there are any specials going on during your vacation to WDW. The Disney travel agent may only tell you about a special if you ask.

One special Disney occasionally offers is free dining. The free dining offer usually occurs during the end of August and at other times during the year. Ask the Disney representative to see when free dining may be going on. This special is especially helpful during one of the school breaks because prices are higher during this time of year.

Disney typically offers other deals throughout the year. An example could be 25% off rooms or some other discounted offer. However, Disney does not discount every room on property. The deal is always on select rooms and some resorts may not be included.

You now need to decide how many days you will be vacationing in Walt Disney World. You use that number to choose the amount of days you want to spend in the theme parks. You can then make the correct selection for your theme park tickets. These tickets are called **Magic Your Way tickets.**

Magic Your Way tickets are the tickets you need to get into the Walt Disney World theme parks. Disney allows you to plan your vacation anyway you like. Magic Your Way Base tickets allow you access to one theme park per day. You can choose to add the park hopping option to your Magic Your Way ticket. This option allows you to go in and out of all of the four theme parks as much as possible. You can buy one day hopper tickets or up to ten day park hopper tickets.

You can also add the water park fun & more option. This option offers a number of visits based on the length of your Magic Your Way ticket. For example, if you purchase a five day Magic Your Way ticket you will give five visits. This will give you access to Blizzard Beach, Typhoon Lagoon, ESPN Wide World of Sports Complex, Disney's nine hole Oak Trail Golf Course, one round of miniature golf at Fantasia Gardens, one round of miniature golf at Winter Summerland, and Disney Quest, which will be closing to become the NBA Experience.

What you decide to buy or not to buy will cause the price per day to change. For example, the difference in price between a four day adult ticket and a seven day adult ticket is only $30. The longer you stay in Walt Disney World, the cheaper it is per day.

The current ticket pricing information as of January 2016, for an Adult Magic Your Way Base ticket (ages 10 and up) that will expire 14 days after first use is:

- 2 day Adult Magic Your Way Base ticket costs $192

- 3 day Adult Magic Your Way Base ticket costs $275
- 4 day Adult Magic Your Way Base ticket costs $305
- 5 day Adult Magic Your Way Base ticket costs $315
- 6 day Adult Magic Your Way Base ticket costs $325
- 7 day Adult Magic Your Way Base ticket costs $335
- 8 day Adult Magic Your Way Base ticket costs $345
- 9 day Adult Magic Your Way Base ticket costs $355
- 10 day Adult Magic Your Way Base ticket costs $365

The current ticket pricing information for a Child Magic Your Way Base ticket (ages 3-9) that will expire 14 days after first use is:

- 2 day Child Magic Your Way Base ticket costs $179
- 3 day Child Magic Your Way Base ticket costs $256
- 4 day Child Magic Your Way Base ticket costs $285
- 5 day Child Magic Your Way Base ticket costs $295
- 6 day Child Magic Your Way Base ticket costs $305
- 7 day Child Magic Your Way Base ticket costs $315
- 8 day Child Magic Your Way Base ticket costs $325
- 9 day Child Magic Your Way Base ticket costs $335
- 10 day Child Magic Your Way Base ticket costs $345

If you decide to add the Water Park Fun & More Option, then add an additional $64 to the base ticket price. If you decide to park hop, which I would recommend, you would add $50 to a Magic Your Way base ticket that is three days or less and $64 to a four or more day Magic Your Way base ticket. If you want to park hop and choose the water park fun & more option it will add an additional $90 to the base ticket price. Please note that the ticket prices do not include tax.

There are some other tidbits of information to consider. An adult one day Magic Kingdom ticket is $105 and a child ticket is $99. An adult one day Epcot, Disney's Hollywood Studios, or Disney's Animal Kingdom ticket is $97 and a child ticket is $91. These one day ticket prices do not include tax. A child under three years of age gets in free.

If you are staying outside of WDW, I would recommend purchasing your Magic Your Way tickets before you arrive. You can purchase them online at disneyworld.com, when you call Disney directly, or through me.

I would not wait until you arrive at a theme park. The reason is the kids and even the adults will want to get in the theme park. They will be very upset when they have to wait in a long line just to buy tickets, while everyone else is entering the park.

In addition to the family being annoyed with you for not purchasing the tickets ahead of time, it will also affect your FastPass+ selections. As I mentioned earlier, you will not be able to make any FastPass+ selections without the Magic Your Way tickets.

If your family enjoys to eat in a sit down restaurant or a buffet once a day or so, you should invest in a **Disney Dining Plan**. The Disney Dining Plan I recommend consists of one snack, one counter service meal, one table service meal per person per amount of nights of your stay in a Walt Disney World Resort, and a resort refillable mug for everyone. It is called the Magic Your Way plus Dining plan.

A snack is almost anything that is around $5.00. A counter service meal is a meal, non-alcoholic drink, and dessert in a Walt Disney World walk up style eatery. An example would be ordering a cheeseburger, fries, coke, and chocolate cake. Tax is also included in the meal.

The dining plan costs $61.84 per adult per night and $20.96 per child per night. These prices include tax. A child is anyone ages 3 to 9. Children under age three eat free at buffets and family style restaurants.

Table service meals provide you an option to eat in any of Disney's sit down restaurants or buffets. If it is a buffet, then it includes the buffet, a non-alcoholic drink, and tax. If the restaurant is a traditional sit down restaurant, then the Disney Dining plan includes your non-alcoholic drink, entree, dessert, and tax per person. You will have to take care of the tip out of your own pocket.

There are a few other dining plans you could choose. The first is called the Disney Quick Service Dining plan. The plan includes two quick service meals and one snack per person, per night of your stay in WDW. The plan also includes a resort refillable mug for everyone. The plan costs $42.84 per adult per night and $17.47 per child per night. The prices include tax.

Another dining plan is the Disney Deluxe Dining plan. This plan includes any type of three meals you choose, two snacks, and a resort refillable mug per person per night in WDW. The plan costs $111.73 per adult per night and $32.56 per child per night. These prices include tax.

Disney now allows you to make certain substitutions within the dining plans. At a table service location you can substitute your dessert for a fruit plate, side salad, or a cup of soup. For this to occur it must be requested. You can substitute one quick service meal for up to three snack items too.

An important piece of information to remember is always check the bottom of your receipt after you have redeemed any dining credits in WDW. There will be a print out of how many credits remain for the type of meal that was redeemed. For example, if you purchased two snacks with your dining plan the bottom of the receipt will show the number of snacks remaining.

When you are ready to make dining reservations you must call 1-407-WDW-DINE or you can make them online at disneyworld.com. You can begin to call or do this online 180 days in advance, and I especially recommend this during the school break weeks. Restaurants fill up quickly. If you are staying on WDW property, then you can call 180 days in advance and book reservations up to 10 days into your vacation.

The dining reservations system is slightly flawed. For

example, when you call or book online, you may be not able to get a reservation at Crystal Palace for a party of four at 6pm. If you ask for two tables of two, they may find availability for you. Yes, you may be seated at different tables, but when you check in at the podium, the hostess will try to make it possible for the entire party of four to sit together.

Disney sometimes has a problem with their dining system when trying to get a table of three. Their system may tell the dining reservation representative for Disney that there are no tables available, but if you ask for a table of four, there may be one available. Basically, I would encourage you to keep trying different scenarios if you are having a problem getting reservations, and one should eventually work. The best fail-safe way to make sure you get the dining reservations you want is to book as close to the 180 day mark as possible.

When you make a dining reservation you need a credit card number to guarantee the reservation at all WDW table service restaurants. Your card will not be charged, but if you need to cancel, do so at least a day in advance. If you do not show up for the reservation and did not cancel it, then Disney will charge your card $10 per person.

The following dining locations also require a credit card number and your card will be charged the full amount of the meal immediately unless you are on a Disney dining plan. The locations are: Cinderella's Royal Table, Spirit of Aloha Dinner

Show, Hoop-Dee-Doo Musical Revue, and Mickey's Backyard BBQ. You can still cancel at least a day in advance and get a full refund.

Mickey's Backyard BBQ

If you have any little girls going on the trip with you, or any little girls at heart, then you **NEED** to make a reservation at Cinderella's Royal Table in Cinderella's Castle. This is located in the Magic Kingdom theme park. When I write the word **"NEED"** I mean this in the strongest way possible. It is an amazing experience you will not want to miss.

It starts off with you walking into Cinderella's Castle and checking in at the podium. They take you inside to have your picture taken with Cinderella and sometimes the Fairy Godmother. When your name is called, you are taken into the dining area which is up a stairwell of winding stairs. The restaurant is beautiful with amazing architecture and it overlooks Fantasyland. You have a spectacular view out of the huge windows that line one whole wall of the dining room. During your meal, many different princesses are on hand and come to the tables to sign autographs, take pictures, and talk with the children.

If you decide to book a reservation to eat in Cinderella's Castle with the princesses you need to start calling or book online 180 days in advance. This restaurant usually books 180 days in advance by 7:30am. Once again, the Disney World dining number is **1-407-WDW-DINE (1-407-939-3463).**

Here is the procedure I recommend. The Walt Disney World dining phone lines open daily at 7am, and the online reservation system begins taking reservations at 6am. If you decide to call, you need to get a credit card because it will be required to hold the reservation.

Next, start calling the dining number at 6:55am. When you first call at 6:55am the recording will say it is closed. You then need to hang up and press redial immediately. Continue to press redial and hang up until the recording says, "Thank you for calling Disney dining. We're glad you called. Your call may be monitored or recorded for quality and training purposes."

The recording will then say, "Which of these dining options would you like? You can say reservations…." Now, immediately say "reservations." The recording will continue and say, “What exactly would you like to do? You can say make a new reservation….” You will say, “New reservation.” The recording will state, “Sure I can help you with that.” You will then say, “Representative.” The recording will say, “Are you currently in the Orlando area or calling about a reservation within the next 7 days?” You will next say, “No,” and you will be connected to the next available Disney representative.

When a dining representative does answer the phone tell them you want breakfast, lunch, or dinner in Cinderella’s Castle, the date, time, and number of people in your party.

Four other restaurants that I would highly recommend booking 180 days in advance of your vacation are: Be Our Guest Restaurant, Chef Mickey's, Hoop Dee Doo Review, and Crystal Palace. Begin calling before 7am or book online at disneyworld.com. They book up very quickly as well. I will go into great detail about WDW restaurants that I recommend in the next chapter.

One dining package your family may want to take advantage of is the **Fantasmic Dining Package.** Fantasmic is an astonishing night time show that takes place in Disney's Hollywood Studios. You have to arrive at least an hour before the show begins, and that still does not guarantee you a seat. You can avoid this by calling Disney dining and reserve this package. When you purchase the package you will be guaranteed seats for your family in the Fantasmic show. You only have to get to the show about 30 minutes before it begins.

The package works at three restaurants in Disney's Hollywood Studios. They are: Hollywood & Vine, Mama Melrose, and the Hollywood Brown Derby.

The Fantasmic Dining Package is available for lunch and dinner at the Hollywood Brown Derby, Hollywood & Vine, and Mama Melrose.

The one downfall of the Fantasmic Dining Package is that you will have restrictions on the times you have to eat. Your dining reservation for lunch usually is between 11:15am and noon. The reservation time for dinner is usually before 4:30pm, but not always.

If you purchase the dining plan I recommended, then Hollywood & Vine and Mama Melrose will be one table service per person and the Hollywood Brown Derby will be two table services per person from the dining plan. However, you do need a credit card to guarantee the package. If you need to cancel at a later date, it would have to be done 48 hours in advance to avoid a $10 per person charge to your credit card.

The Hollywood Brown Derby

Chapter 5

Dining Recommendations

I highly recommend eating in at least one of Disney's character dining restaurants. This is a great experience for the whole family, and it is a huge time saver. You can see the characters you want, get autographs, and take pictures with the characters during the meal. If you get autographs and pictures with the characters in the theme parks, it could take up to twenty minutes or more **per character.**

The following are restaurants I highly recommend in Walt Disney World. The prices that are listed are for the restaurants that have a buffet or serve family style. The prices are per person for adults and children and include tax.

These are the prices you will have to pay if you are **not** using a Disney dining plan, especially the one I recommended. If you are on the dining plan, you then will use your table service credits. You will notice that it is very expensive to eat in Walt Disney World without the dining plan.

Table Service Restaurants Recommended (Magic Kingdom)

1) Cinderella's Royal Table (Character Dining) - All you can eat breakfast, lunch, or dinner with Cinderella and other princesses inside Cinderella's Castle. However, it is not a buffet. Your server will bring you as many plates as you want. My family and I have created wonderful memories in the Castle. I still remember my daughter, at age three, being dressed up as Snow White and Snow White herself came over and spoke with her. Megan absolutely lit up. **Pricing:** Adults range from $55.81 to $75.83. Children range from $34.71 to $45.24. (**Note:** It is two table service credits per person from the dining plan.) **Directions:** After you have entered the Magic Kingdom walk down Main Street and you will see the Castle in the distance. Walk towards it and go through the middle of it. On your right you will see the entrance for the restaurant.

2) **Crystal Palace (Character Dining)** - A buffet is served for breakfast, lunch, or dinner with Pooh Bear and his friends. The restaurant is beautiful. It has windows everywhere, and from the outside it looks like you are eating in an enormous crystal ball. This is one of my favorite restaurants in WDW. Your children can even participate in a parade with the characters around the restaurant. **Pricing:** Adults range from $24.99 to $43.66. Children range from $13.99 to $24.29. **Directions:** After you have entered the Magic Kingdom walk down Main Street past the shops. Keep looking to the left and take the first walkway you see on your left. That will lead you to the Crystal Palace.

Welcome sign inside of Crystal Palace

3) **Liberty Tree Tavern** – The restaurant is family style for dinner with American Thanksgiving style foods. During lunch there is a regular menu that includes: New England clam chowder, pot roast, cheeseburger, BLT, and roast turkey. **Pricing:** Adults range from $31.99 to $38.33. Children range from $15.99 to $19.16. **Directions:** Make your way over to Liberty Square, which is to the left of the Castle. Walk past the Hall of Presidents on your right and take your first left. The restaurant will be directly on your left.

4) **Tony's Town Square Restaurant** – Authentic Italian food with a theme from the movie "Lady and the Tramp."

Directions: After you enter the Magic Kingdom the restaurant will be on the right next to the Town Square Theater.

5) Be Our Guest Restaurant – You will be immersed in the world of "Beauty and the Beast." After you enter, you will encounter suits of armor in the hallway that actually speak. You and your family will eat in the Beast's castle in three different dining rooms, one being the mysterious West Wing. Breakfast is quick service dining and includes: bacon and egg sandwich, eggs Florentine, and a croissant doughnut. During lunch the restaurant is quick service style dining serving scrumptious sandwiches. The restaurant is table service for dinner and the menu features pork rack chops, salmon, strip steak, scallops, and shrimp. I highly recommend making a dining reservation for any meal.
Directions: Walk through the Castle and enter Fantasyland. Keep walking straight and enter the "new" Fantasyland. The restaurant will be on your left.

Entrance to Be Our Guest restaurant

Table Service Restaurants Recommended

(Disney's Hollywood Studios)

1) Hollywood & Vine (Character dining) - An all you can eat breakfast or lunch buffet with Jake, Handy Manny, Doc McStuffins, and Princess Sofia the First from Disney Junior. Dinner is offered too and you will be joined by Minnie, Mickey, Donald, Daisy, and Goofy for dinner celebrations centered on the different seasons of the year. This is called Minnie's seasonal dining. **Pricing:** Adults range from $26.62 to $46.99. Children range from $15.97 to $29.99. **Directions:** After you have entered the Studios walk past the shops and take the first open walkway on your left. The restaurant will be down on the left.

Hollywood & Vine

2) **Mama Melrose's Ristorante Italiano** – This is a tasty sit down Italian restaurant. The delicious Italian specialties include: brick oven pizzas, steak, pasta, and chicken. **Directions:** Make your way over to the Muppets. Go to the left of the Muppets attraction and your destination will be slightly on the left.

Mama Melrose

3) **50s Prime Time Café** – A feel like home sit down type restaurant. You can have all types of comfort foods just like being in grandma's house. Make sure not to have your elbows on the table. Specialties include fried chicken, pot roast, and meatloaf. **Directions:** After you have entered the Studios walk past the

shops and take the first open walkway on your left. The restaurant will be down on the left.

50s Prime Time Café

4) **The Hollywood Brown Derby** – An upscale sit down restaurant themed after the famous restaurant in Hollywood. The Brown Derby serves steak, chicken, roasted rack of lamb, Cobb salad, and salmon. It is expensive, and does require 2 Table Services if you are on the dining plan I recommended. **Directions:** After you have entered the Studios walk straight ahead. Just after the first walkway on your right you will see the Brown Derby on your right.

5) **Sci - Fi Restaurant** – This sit down restaurant

resembles an old drive in Movie Theater. You actually sit in a car, and there is a large screen playing old Sci - Fi movie clips. The ceiling looks like the night sky with stars everywhere. The menu includes: burgers, steaks, pasta, sandwiches, ribs, and shakes. The downside is that the restaurant is dark. **Directions:** After you enter the Studios walk towards the Great Movie Ride. You then will go to the left and follow the walkway. You will walk by the ABC Commissary and the restaurant is on the right.

Sci-Fi Restaurant

Table Service Restaurants Recommended (Disney's Animal Kingdom)

1) **Donald's Safari Breakfast, Lunch, & Dinner at the Tusker House Restaurant (Character dining)** – A breakfast,

lunch, & dinner buffet with Donald, Mickey, and friends. The breakfast features everything from scrambled eggs to cheese blintzes and all foods in-between. Lunch and dinner includes carved meats, rotisserie chicken, and numerous other choices. Your child can even participate in a parade around the restaurant. **Pricing:** Adults range from $29.99 to $41.99. Children range from $17.99 to $24.99. **Directions:** Walk towards the Africa section and enter Africa. The restaurant will be on your left.

Inside the Tusker House

2) **Yak & Yeti Restaurant** – This restaurant serves Asian cuisine including salmon, honey chicken, tempura shrimp, and sweet and sour pork. **Directions:** Walk towards Asia and the Flights of Wonder will be on your left. Keep going and the restaurant will be on your left.

Table Service Restaurants Recommended (Epcot)

1) **Le Cellier Steakhouse** – A superb steakhouse in the Canada Pavilion of Epcot. The filet mignon is incredible and melts in your mouth. Lunch and dinner are two Table Services if you are on the dining plan. **Directions:** Make your way over to the Canada section of Epcot, which is located in World Showcase. As you enter Canada, Le Cellier will be on your right.

Le Cellier

2) Tutto Italia Ristorante (Italy Pavilion) – Tutto Italia serves authentic Italian food. You will experience the feel of Italy while eating dishes such as: calamari, lasagna, homemade pastas, and pork chops. **Directions:** Make your way over to the Italy section of Epcot, which is located in World Showcase. When you finally get into Italy, the restaurant will be on your right across from the lagoon.

3) **Coral Reef Restaurant (The Seas with Nemo & Friends Pavilion)** – You will eat mouthwatering seafood, steaks, and pasta dishes while watching sea life in a huge aquarium. Ask to be seated in front of the aquarium, and you may even get lucky and see a scuba diver in the tank! **Directions:** As you enter Epcot, walk to the right of Spaceship Earth. Follow the first walkway to the right and make your way to The Seas with Nemo & Friends attraction. Go to the right of it and the restaurant will be on your left.

4) **Nine Dragons Restaurant (China Pavilion)** – The restaurant has great Chinese food and you can get almost anything you can imagine. Some menu choices include: shrimp and chicken egg rolls, honey-sesame chicken, sweet and sour pork, and vegetable stir fry. **Directions:** Make your way over to China in World Showcase and the restaurant will be on your left.

5) **Teppan Edo (Japan Pavilion)** – Teppan Edo serves magnificent Japanese food in a restaurant that is one of a kind. You will be entertained at your table as chefs prepare stir-fry, shellfish, meats, and vegetables right in front of you. **Directions:** As you enter the Japan Pavilion look for a building on your left with numerous stairs. Go up the stairs to enter the restaurant.

Stairs leading to Teppan Edo

6) Akershus Royal Banquet Hall (Character dining) – This is a stunning experience while eating breakfast, lunch, or dinner with the Disney princesses. It is a medieval castle style restaurant in the Norway Pavilion. Breakfast is a buffet, while lunch and dinner are served family style. **Pricing:** Adults range from $40.46 to $55.37. Children range from $24.49 to $29.81. **Directions:** Take your family over to the Norway Pavilion in World Showcase and the restaurant will be on your left.

7) **Rose and Crown Pub and Dining Room** – The Rose and Crown is a friendly British pub located in the United Kingdom Pavilion of Epcot. It offers tradition British food and drinks. The food specialties include: fish and chips, bangers and

mash, corned beef and cabbage, and Shepherd's pie. There is even outdoor seating with a piano player. **Directions:** Make your way over to the United Kingdom Pavilion in World Showcase. After you walk through Canada the restaurant will be on your left.

Rose and Crown Pub

8) **Via Napoli (Italy Pavilion)** – This authentic Italian restaurant serves mouthwatering dishes. Some of the menu highlights include: homemade pasta, chicken, eggplant, veal parmesan, and wood fire authentic pizzas. **Directions:** Make your way over to the Italy section of Epcot, which is located in World Showcase. When you finally get into Italy, the restaurant will be on your right across from the lagoon.

Table Service Restaurants Recommended (Walt Disney World Resorts)

1) **Chef Mickey's at Disney's Contemporary Resort (Character Dining)** – Everyone needs to get ready to wave their napkin in the air at this breakfast, lunch, and dinner buffet with Mickey and friends! This is a very popular restaurant that books up very quickly. Call to make the reservation 180 days in advance. Breakfast items include Mickey waffles, scrambled eggs, and breakfast meats. For lunch & dinner, carved meats, pasta dishes, homemade mashed potatoes, and much, much more are served. My family always looks forward to eating with Mickey and taking a picture with him. **Pricing:** Adults range from \$36.01 to \$52.05. Children range from \$19.10 to \$29.55. **Directions:** The resort is next to the Magic Kingdom. Enter the resort and take the elevators to the 4th floor.

Chef Mickey's

2) **Cape May at Disney's Beach Club Resort** – This is my favorite restaurant in WDW. Your family will enjoy a seafood/clam bake and American buffet for dinner or a character breakfast buffet with Mickey, Minnie, and Friends in the morning. **Pricing:** Adults range from $26.62 to $59.59. Children range from $14.84 to $22.99**. Directions:** The resort is located next to the Yacht Club on the Boardwalk. After you enter the resort, go to your right and you will see the restaurant entrance.

3) **Boma at Disney's Animal Kingdom Lodge (Jambo House)** – Boma is an incredible breakfast and dinner buffet featuring all types of African foods. The desserts are to die for. Try the Zebra domes! **Pricing:** Adults range from $20.23 to $42.59. Children range from $11.71 to $21.29. **Directions:** The resort is located near Disney's Animal Kingdom theme park. You will enter the Jambo House building and take the stairs down and the restaurant will be on your left.

Boma

4) **1900 Park Fare at Disney's Grand Floridian Resort & Spa (Character Dining)** – A buffet featuring numerous items to choose from for breakfast and dinner. Mary Poppins, The Mad Hatter, and others are available for breakfast and Cinderella, Prince Charming, and others are available for dinner. Some of the highlights are lobster eggs benedict and smoked salmon for breakfast, and pasta and a carving station for dinner. **Pricing:** Adults range from $25.36 to $45.50. Children range from $15.77 to $26.99. **Directions:** The resort is in the Magic Kingdom resort area. After you enter through the front doors you will be in the lobby, which is spectacular! Make your way over to the left and you will see the restaurant sign.

5) **Narcoossee's at Disney's Grand Floridian Resort & Spa** – This is a signature dining restaurant featuring incredibly fresh seafood. The menu features two pound whole Maine lobster, scallops, filet mignon, tuna, and Black Angus New York strip steak. However, the restaurant is very expensive. The filet mignon is priced at around $49 and the whole Maine lobster runs for about $72. **Directions:** After you enter the resort you will walk through the main building out the back doors. Go slightly to your left and you will walk by building six and seven. The restaurant is to the right of building seven.

6) **Hoop Dee Doo Musical Revue at Disney's Fort Wilderness** – This interactive dinner show is very entertaining for the whole family. The show times are: 4pm, 6:15pm, and

8:30pm. The food is served family style and you enjoy fried chicken, ribs, cornbread, mashed potatoes, beans, and strawberry shortcake. It does require 2 table services. You will have to pick up the tickets for the show at your resort. My children loved all the silly jokes, the actors, and actresses. **Pricing:** Adults range from $61.99 to $67.99 depending on where your party sits. Children range from $36.99 to $39.99. **Directions:** You will take a boat from the Magic Kingdom to the resort. After you exit the boat, you will follow the signs to the Hoop Dee Doo Musical Revue which will be straight ahead. It is located in Pioneer Hall.

7) **Beaches and Cream Soda Shop at Disney's Beach Club Resort** – A 50s style diner featuring burgers, hot dogs, and amazing sundaes. They do now take reservations. If you just want to grab a cone or a sundae, they do have a walk up window. I highly recommend the No Way Jose sundae, which features hot fudge and peanut butter! **Directions:** The Beach Club is in the Epcot resort area on the Boardwalk. You will enter the resort and go to your right. You will see Cape May on your right and follow the walkway around the entire restaurant. Take a right out the doors and Beaches and Cream will be directly across from the pool on your right.

8) **'Ohana at Disney's Polynesian Village Resort** – 'Ohana is a Hawaiian themed restaurant that has family style dining for a character breakfast with Mickey, Lilo, and Stitch. Expect to be greeted with a lei and take a family photo.

Scrambled eggs, warm breads, Mickey waffles, and sausage are served for breakfast. Dinner is also served family style. Pork fried dumplings, sirloin steak, and grilled peel and eat shrimp are on the dinner menu. **Pricing:** Adults range from $28.36 to $44.59. Children range from $16.77 to $25.23. **Directions:** The Polynesian Village Resort is a Magic Kingdom area resort. After you enter the resort, you can take the stairs or the elevators to the second floor, which is where the restaurant is located.

9) **Captain's Grille at Disney's Yacht Club Resort** – Captain's Grille is a beautiful elegant restaurant serving breakfast, lunch, and dinner. You can order off the menu for breakfast or opt for the buffet. The menu has numerous choices such as: New England clam chowder, crab legs, steak, crab cakes, and so much more for lunch or dinner. Your bill will add up if you are not on the dining plan. **Directions:** The resort is part of the Epcot resort area. Enter the resort and it is located on the left side of the lobby.

Captain's Grille

10) **ESPN Club at Disney's Boardwalk area** – This is the place for all the sports fans in your family! You can watch your favorite team right here while on vacation. The restaurant serves lunch and dinner. You can have a huge burger, salad, nachos, chili, hot dog, chicken, and even a steak. On certain nights, you can be part of a live show. They do not take reservations, so you may have a short wait for a table.
Directions: Make your way over to Disney's Boardwalk Resort. Go to the back of the resort and out the back doors. Take a right onto the Boardwalk. Follow the walkway and the restaurant will be the last building on your right.

ESPN Club

11) **Big River Grille and Brewing Works at Disney's Boardwalk area** – The restaurant makes their own specialty beers and has delicious food. They serve: beer cheese soup, cheeseburgers, Mahi Mahi, chicken alfredo, meatloaf, and steaks, just to name a few. You can even sit outside if the mood strikes you. **Directions:** Go to Disney's Boardwalk Resort. Go to the back of the resort and out the back doors. Take a left onto the Boardwalk. The restaurant will be on your left.

12) **Spirit of Aloha Dinner Show at Disney's Polynesian Village Resort** – Come and join the party that features music and dances at this one of a kind luau. You will feast on pork ribs, roasted chicken, salads, breads, rice, seasonal vegetables, and desserts. It will take 2 table service credits from the dining plan I recommended. There are two shows Tuesday – Saturday at 5:15 and 8pm and they book up very quickly. You will have to pick up the tickets for the show at your resort or at the Polynesian. **Pricing:** Adults range from $60.99 - $73.99 and children range from $33.99 to $39.99. The price range is large because it depends on your seating area. **Directions:** Enter the Polynesian Village Resort and follow the signs for Luau Cove.

13) **California Grill at Disney's Contemporary Resort** – This restaurant serves outstanding California style food for brunch and dinner. The brunch menu contains buttermilk chicken cutlet, sweet potato pancakes, shrimp and grits, lobster benedict, frittata, and so much more. The brunch costs $80 for adults and

$48 for children. The menu for dinner includes: sushi, pork, Atlantic flounder, scallops, lamb porterhouse, and many other choices. You are able to see the Magic Kingdom fireworks from certain areas of the restaurant. Please note that you will check in for dinner on the 2nd floor next to the escalators. **Directions:** The resort is next to the Magic Kingdom. After you enter the resort, the restaurant is located on the 15th floor.

14) **Trail's End Restaurant in Disney's Fort Wilderness** – The Trail's End restaurant is a very good overall price if you are paying out of pocket. It has a warm cabin theme feel and it is a buffet for breakfast and dinner. The breakfast buffet includes: warm pecan cinnamon buns, plain or chocolate chip Mickey waffles, eggs benedict with ham or pulled pork, breakfast pizza, and other traditional breakfast items. The dinner buffet contains: shrimp, ribs, fried chicken, pasta, fish, and carved meats. For lunch you will order off the menu featuring: chicken and waffles, chicken fried steak, catfish, shrimp and grits, and cheeseburgers. There are no characters for any of the meals. **Pricing:** Adults range from $17.99 to $26.62 and children range from $9.99 to $15.90. **Directions:** You will take a boat from the Magic Kingdom to the resort. After you exit the boat, you will walk straight ahead and follow the path. It is next to the Hoop Dee Doo Revue.

Trail's End Restaurant

15) **The Wave of American Flavors at Disney's Contemporary Resort** – You will have a quiet dining experience as you feast on delicious food in this contemporary restaurant. You have the choice of the buffet or ordering off the menu for breakfast. The buffet items include: traditional breakfast items, Mickey waffles, eggs benedict, oatmeal, sweet potato pancakes, and more. The lunch and dinner menus are a la carte. Lunch items include: bacon, lobster, lettuce, and tomato club, Reuben, grilled chicken breast, and burgers. Dinner items include: lamb shank, grilled fish, beef short ribs, and pork tenderloin. **Pricing:** Adults $21.49 and children $$11.99 for the breakfast buffet. **Directions:** Enter the Contemporary Resort and walk by the front desk which will be on your left. The restaurant is at the end of the

front desk on your left.

Table Service Restaurants Recommended (Disney Springs)

1) **T – Rex** – Dinosaurs are king and everywhere in this one of a kind restaurant. An asteroid show occurs approximately every 30 minutes. The restaurant has large portion sizes which include burgers, chicken, pasta, seafood, salads, and much more. The easiest way to make a reservation at this restaurant is to call them directly. Their direct number is (407) 828-8739.

Directions: Enter Disney Springs' Marketplace and T-Rex is to the right of Planet Hollywood. Look for the large dinosaur and the T-Rex sign.

2) **Fulton's Crab House** – You will have the chance to feast on crab cakes, oysters, crab and lobster bisque, New England clam chowder, lobster, steaks, and so much more.

Directions: Enter Disney Springs' Marketplace and make your way over to T-Rex. Walk past T-Rex and then go to the left. The restaurant is anchored in the water.

Magic Kingdom walk up dining suggestions (counter service)

1) **Cosmic Ray's Starlight Café** (Tomorrowland) – This counter service location serves burgers, Rotisserie chicken, BBQ pork

sandwiches, chicken and ribs combos, chicken nuggets, and hot dogs in three different walk up areas called Bays. You can even listen to Sunny Eclipse sing on stage.

Starlight Café

2) **Columbia Harbour House** (Liberty Square) - Fish, chicken, New England clam chowder, lobster roll, grilled salmon, and seasonal cobbler are the specialties in this family favorite.

Columbia Harbour House

3) **Be Our Guest Restaurant** (New Fantasyland) - Carved turkey, prime roast beef, and braised pork sandwiches are delicious and available for lunch. Breakfast meals include bacon and egg sandwich, eggs Florentine, and a croissant doughnut.

4) **Pecos Bill Tall Tale Inn and Café** (Frontierland) – The menu has undergone an overhaul and now serves southwest chicken salads, steak or chicken fajita platters, beef or chicken burritos, and a variety of rice bowls.

Pecos Bill's

5) **Pinocchio Village Haus** (Fantasyland) – Flatbread pizzas, chicken Alfredo, chicken parmesan, chicken nuggets, and Caesar salad with chicken can be found in this counter service location.

6) **Gaston's Tavern** (New Fantasyland) – You can take a load off in Gaston's Tavern and partake in warm cinnamon rolls, chocolate croissants, Tavern beef stew, and LeFou's Brew which is frozen apple juice with a hint of toasted marshmallow. Gaston may even make an appearance in front of the tavern.

Gaston's Tavern

7) **Casey's Corner** (Main Street) – If you want to grab a hot dog, then this is the location to make a pit stop. Fries and nachos are served as well.

8) **The Diamond Horseshoe** (Liberty Square) - Turkey sandwiches, pork brisket sandwiches, BBQ chicken sandwiches, and salads can be found in this quick service location, which is open seasonally.

Disney's Animal Kingdom walk up dining suggestions (counter service)

1) **Restaurantosaurus** (Dinoland) – This personal favorite of

mine has bacon cheeseburgers, macaroni and cheese hot dogs, grilled chicken sandwiches, and chicken nuggets.

Restaurantosaurus

2) **Flame Tree Barbecue** (Discovery Island) – When you are in the mood for barbeque then stop by the Flame Tree. You can get up to your armpits in ribs, chicken, pulled pork sandwiches, and turkey breast sandwiches.

3) **Pizzafari** (Discovery Island) – This counter service location serves some wonderful meals that include: cheese, pepperoni, or meat lover's pizza and meatball subs.

Pizzafari

4) **Harambe Market** (Africa) – This authentic food market has delicious food choices. A few of them are: grilled chicken skewer, gyro flatbread, sausages, and ribs.

5) **Yak & Yeti Local Food Cafes** (Asia) – If you escape from the Yeti after riding Expedition Everest, then stop by to grab a taste of honey chicken, egg rolls, teriyaki beef bowls, and Asian chicken sandwiches.

Disney's Hollywood Studios walk up dining suggestions (counter service)

1) **Backlot Express** - Bacon cheeseburgers, chili hot dogs, chicken nuggets, chicken & waffles, and salads can be found at

this counter service location that contains Hollywood memorabilia.

Backlot Express

2) **Toy Story Pizza Planet –** If you are a Toy Story fan that you have to check out Pizza Planet. You can order cheese, vegetable, pepperoni, or meat lover's pizzas, Caesar salads, and meatball subs.

Pizza Planet

3) **Rosie's All-American Café** – You can feast on cheeseburgers and chicken nuggets in this outdoor quick service location. It is only steps away from the Tower of Terror.

4) **ABC Commissary** – This counter service location has a wide range of food choices which include: Asian salads with chicken or salmon, cheeseburgers, shrimp, fish, New York strip steak, and chicken club sandwiches.

5) **Catalina Eddie's** – You can grab pizzas, Caesar salads with chicken, and hot Italian deli sandwiches from this outdoor location that is located next to Rosie's All-American Café. You can check out a Beauty and the Beast show after your meal since it is only a stone's throw away.

Epcot walk up dining suggestions (counter service)

1) **Electric Umbrella** (Future World East) – This is a wonderful location for a quick lunch or dinner. There are numerous seating areas including outside and upstairs. The menu has bacon cheeseburgers, vegetable flatbreads, chicken nuggets, sausage and pepper sandwiches, and salad with roasted chicken.

2) **Sunshine Seasons** (Land Pavilion) – Sunshine Seasons is a food court with a wide variety of food choices for breakfast, lunch, or dinner. Some of the selections include: breakfast platters, breakfast Paninis, Asian foods, salads, pork chops, chicken, and sandwiches.

Sunshine Seasons

3) **La Cantina de San Angel** (Mexico Pavilion) – As you stroll through the Mexico Pavilion make sure you stop by to sample tacos, empanadas, and nachos.

4) **Lotus Blossom Café** (China Pavilion) – This walk up style eatery has luscious egg rolls, shrimp fried rice, vegetable curry over rice, and orange chicken.

Lotus Blossom Café

5) **Liberty Inn** (American Adventure Pavilion) - Bacon cheeseburgers, steak, shrimp, chicken nuggets, hot dogs, and salads are the specialties in this quick service location. There is plenty of seating inside and outside in the Florida sun.

6) **Yorkshire County Fish Shop** (United Kingdom Pavilion) – Are you in the mood for authentic fish and chips? Then, walk up and place an order when you are in the United Kingdom Pavilion. It will be worth it!

Yorkshire County Fish Shop

Now that you have an idea of where to make dining reservations, I recommend you plan the theme parks you are going to attend accordingly. For example, if you make a dinner reservation at Chef Mickey's in the Contemporary, make sure you plan on going to the Magic Kingdom that day, since it is right next to the Magic Kingdom theme park. If you make a dinner reservation at the Hollywood Brown Derby, obviously go to Disney's Hollywood Studios that morning. I would recommend attending Disney's Animal Kingdom if you are eating dinner at Boma, since it is located in Disney's Animal Kingdom Lodge.

Chapter 6

MyMagic+, mydisneyexperience.com, FastPass+, MagicBands, & DAS)

Walt Disney World now features their new creation of magic called MyMagic+. MyMagic+ encompasses all of the following: mydisneyexperience.com, FastPass+, the new MagicBands, and the mydisneyexperience app.

After you have booked your vacation package with a travel agent you will visit the website mydisneyexperience.com. On the top of the screen you will click on "create account," and follow the steps to obtain your own account.

The first item on your agenda will be to link your resort reservation package. You will put your cursor on "My Disney Experience" on the top right of the screen, and a drop down menu will appear. You will click on "My Reservations and Tickets." You will then type in your resort reservation number and your last name. Your reservation package will appear in your account.

While you are on the page "My Reservations and Tickets" you will link your dining reservations. It is possible that your dining reservation may appear after you have linked your resort reservation. But, typically this does not occur, however, it is fairly easy to link your dining reservations. All you have to do is click on "Link Dining Reservation." You will type in the confirmation number of a dining reservation and your last name. The reservation will then appear in your account along with all the other dining reservations you have made with Disney dining. Although, if the other dining reservations do not appear then you will type in the confirmation number of another dining reservation and your last name one at a time.

On this same page titled "My Reservations and Tickets" the theme park tickets you have purchased as part of your package will now appear.

However, you will have to link your **Magic Your Way** tickets if you are not staying in a WDW resort. You will click on "Link Tickets" and type in the number on the back of the Magic Your Way ticket. This will now allow you to set up FastPass+. **Please note to order The Magic Your Way tickets a number of months in advance and have them shipped to your house to make sure you have the tickets in your hand.**

The next item on your agenda will be to make FastPass+ selections. FastPass+ is a free service and it is included with your theme park admission. The concept of FastPass+ is a novel one. The service allows you to reserve a place in line at your favorite attractions, while you enjoy other attractions in the theme park. It gives you the option of not standing in a line for ridiculous lengths of time.

You will make FastPass+ selections 60 days before your vacation a few minutes after midnight if you are staying in a Walt Disney World resort. If you are staying off site, you can make FastPass+ selections 30 days in advance.

If you are not purchasing your Magic Your Way tickets until you arrive in WDW, then you can sign up for FastPass+ in the theme parks at a MyMagic+ service center.

Here is how you sign up for FastPass+. While you are in your mydisneyexperience.com account you will scroll over "My Disney Experience" on the top right of the screen. You will click on FastPass+.

You will select "New FastPass+." On the next screen you will choose all the members of your family that will be going on the attractions and then click on "Next" on the bottom of the screen. **Please note to always click on "Next" to move to a new screen while using the website.** A common mistake people make is to forget to click the "Next" button. This will cause issues on certain pages of the website.

You will choose the theme park you are visiting and the date. Many different FastPass+ choices will appear according to the theme park you chose. You will select 3 FastPass+ attractions.

In the Magic Kingdom the attractions that have the FastPass+ option are as follows:

- It's a Small World
- Big Thunder Mountain Railroad
- Buzz Lightyear's Space Ranger Spin
- Disney Festival of Fantasy Parade
- Dumbo

- Enchanted Tales with Belle
- Haunted Mansion
- Jungle Cruise
- Mad Tea Party
- Main Street Electrical Parade
- Meet Anna and Elsa at Princess Fairytale Hall
- Meet Ariel at Ariel's Grotto
- Meet Cinderella and Rapunzel at Princess Fairytale Hall
- Meet Mickey Mouse
- Meet Tinker Bell
- Mickey's PhilharMagic
- Monster's Inc. Laugh Floor
- Peter Pan's Flight
- Pirates of the Caribbean
- Seven Dwarfs Mine Train
- Space Mountain
- Splash Mountain
- The Barnstormer
- The Magic Carpets of Aladdin
- The Many Adventures of Winnie the Pooh
- Tomorrowland Speedway
- Under the Sea - Journey of the Little Mermaid
- Wishes

In Epcot the attractions are placed into two different

categories. In the first category you can choose one FastPass+ attraction from either: Illuminations, Living with the Land, Mission: Space, Soarin, or Test Track.

You can choose two attractions from the second category. The FastPass+ attractions include: Disney & Pixar Short Film Festival, Journey into Imagination with Figment, Meet Disney Pals at the Epcot Character Spot, Spaceship Earth, The Seas with Nemo and Friends, and Turtle Talk with Crush.

If you select Disney's Hollywood Studios you can choose one attraction for FastPass+ from these attractions: Beauty and the Beast, Fantasmic, Great Movie Ride, Rock-n-Roller Coaster, and Toy Story Midway Mania.

Your other two FastPass+ selections can be made from the following attractions: Disney Junior, For the First Time in Forever: A Frozen Sing – Along Celebration, Indiana Jones Epic Stunt Spectacular, Lights Motor Action Extreme Stunt Show, Muppet Vision 3D, Star Tours, The Twilight Zone Tower of Terror, and the Voyage of the Little Mermaid.

In Disney's Animal Kingdom the attractions that have the FastPass+ option are as follows:

- Dinosaur
- Expedition Everest
- Festival of the Lion King
- Finding Nemo – the Musical
- Flights of Wonder

- It's Tough to be a Bug!
- Kali River Rapids
- Kilimanjaro Safaris
- Meet Disney Pals at Adventurers Outpost
- Primeval Whirl

There are a limited number of FastPass+ reservations available for attractions each day. Certain attractions will run out of FastPass+ for the entire day before others. For example, Toy Story Midway Mania in Disney's Hollywood Studios and the Seven Dwarfs Mine Train in the Magic Kingdom, just to name two, will have no more FastPass+ times available possibly 50 days before your vacation. The meet and greet with Anna and Elsa at Princess Fairytale Hall may have no FastPass+ times available by approximately 60 days in advance at 8am. You always have the option of waiting in the standby line for any attraction.

After you have selected three FastPass+ attractions you will be given four different time options. The time options will be an hour window time slot for each FastPass+ attraction. For example, a FastPass+ could be for Space Mountain from 1:00pm – 2:00pm. You will go through each option and select the times that work best for your schedule.

This next point is one that many people overlook. You can easily change one or all of the times you have chosen or you can even change the attraction to a different one. To accomplish this you will click on "Update FastPass+" and the website will have you select the date you want to change the FastPass+ selections. You then can change the FastPass+ experience or time. If you choose to change the time, make sure you click on the word "update" after you are done. This will guarantee that the change has been accomplished.

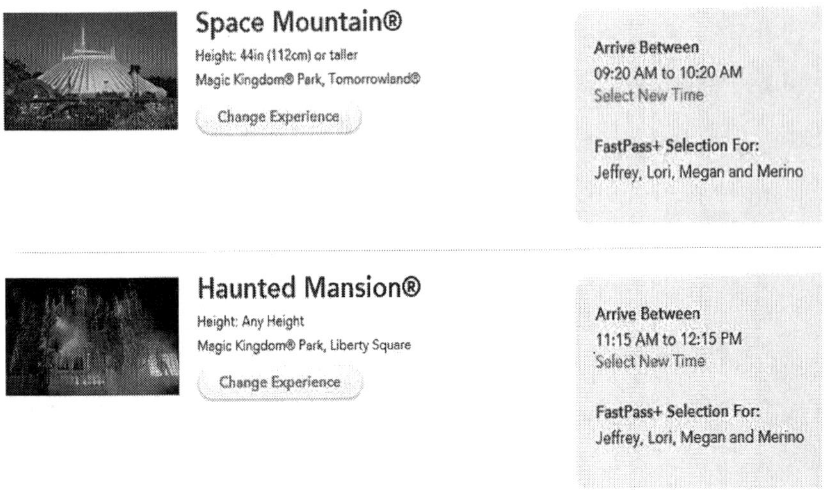

It is now time to choose the MagicBands for your family. Your MagicBand is your "Key to the World." It will act as your Disney's Magical Express ticket for the shuttle, resort room key, theme park ticket, dining plan if one is part of your package, FastPass+ ticket, and charge card.

You can customize your MagicBands by clicking on "MagicBands and Cards" under "MyDisneyExperience" on the top right of the website. You will be able to select different colors for everyone's MagicBand. The MagicBands can have the same color too. It is completely up to you.

You will decide what name is going to appear on the inside of everyone's individual MagicBand. When this is accomplished you will have them shipped directly to your home address. They typically ship just after final payment has been made, which is 30 days in advance.

There are other options you can view from the mydisneyexperience website. You can view your entire itinerary during your vacation. You can adjust information in your account, invite family and friends to view dining reservation or FastPass+ selections, and link the memory maker to your account if you purchased one.

You can also view all photos taken on attractions and by Disney photographers by clicking on "Disney PhotoPass." This can be found under "MyDisneyExperience" at the top of the page.

There is a mydisneyexperience app that is free through the app store. You absolutely need to download it to your smartphone. You will have access to your check-in time for your resort, all of the FastPass+ selections you have made, and your dining reservations.

The app has numerous other advantages. On the bottom of the screen you will see an "addition sign." You can click on it and choose new FastPass+ experiences, modify FastPass+ selections and times, purchase theme park tickets, make or change dining reservations, add parades, fireworks or shows to your plans, and shop for Disney theme park merchandise.

At the top of the app you can view attraction wait times, find your favorite character, locate a restroom, find the location of Disney photographers by clicking on PhotoPass, and almost anything else you need at your disposal.

At the top left of the app you will see three straight lines. Click on the lines and most of the selections discussed above will appear. The choices will be: home, search, buy tickets, buy merchandise, buy memory maker, park hours, wait times, FastPass+, dining, PhotoPass, my reservations, my profile, wish list, notifications, help, and sign out.

When your vacation has finally begun you will enter your first WDW theme park. When you are ready to use your first FastPass+ selection, go to the select attraction during the hour window time slot you have chosen. You need to locate the FastPass+ entrance.

FastPass+ Entrance

You will touch your MagicBand on the Mickey symbol side against the other Mickey symbol. It will light up green and you can then walk through the FastPass+ entrance. If you just have a Magic Your Way ticket, you will touch your ticket to the Mickey symbol. Please note that you will be able to redeem your FastPass+ selection five minutes before it actually begins.

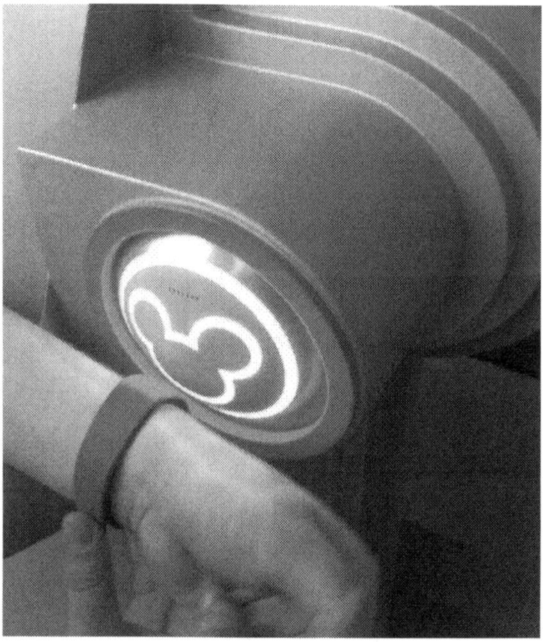

Using your MagicBand for FastPass+

After you have redeemed your three FastPass+ selections, you will be able to make additional FastPass+ choices at the in-park kiosks. There are a few restrictions with this. You can only make one additional FastPass+ selection at a time, if a FastPass+ is available for the select attraction. After you use this new

FastPass+, you can then make another and so on until the FastPass+ selections are no longer available for the day.

You will be able to make these additional FastPass+ selections for any attraction, even if it is an experience you already redeemed a FastPass+ for earlier that day, depending on availability.

After you have used your three FastPass+ selections, you can make additional selections in a different theme park. However, this must be done at a FastPass+ kiosk in the new theme park.

FastPass+ Kiosk

The FastPass+ kiosks are strategically located in each theme park. In the Magic Kingdom the FastPass+ kiosks are located next to Stitch's Great Escape, in front of Mickey's PhilharMagic, between the Diamond Horseshoe and Frontier Trading Post, and next to the Jungle Cruise.

In Epcot the FastPass+ kiosks are located between the Electric Umbrella and MouseGear, between the Character Spot and the walkway to the Land, and in the International Gateway in front of the World Traveler shop.

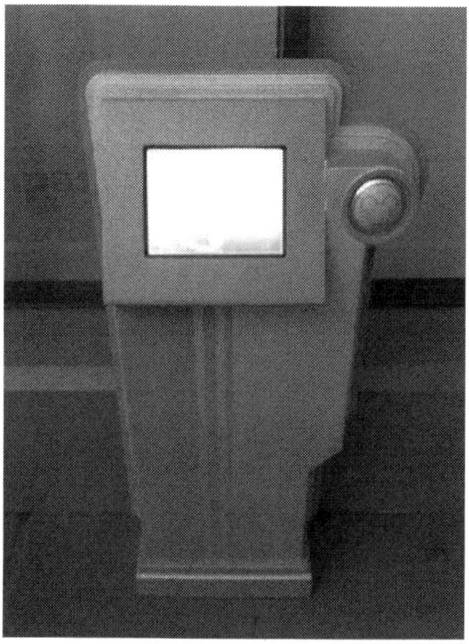

FastPass+ kiosk in Epcot

In Disney's Hollywood Studios the FastPass+ kiosks are located next to Toy Story Midway Mania, on the corner of Hollywood Boulevard and Sunset Boulevard, in front of the Tower of Terror, and to the right of Muppet Vision 3D.

In Disney's Animal Kingdom the FastPass+ kiosks are

located in Africa on the path to the Harambe Market, next to Kali River Rapids in Asia, and there are two across from each other on the main path towards the Tree of Life.

If one of your FastPass+ attractions experiences technical difficulties for an extended period of time you will get a notification in your mydisneyexperience account. You will be able to choose another attraction and use your FastPass+ at that location.

There have been changes to the Disney Guest Access Card. It is now called the **Disability Access Service (DAS).** If your child or someone in your party has a disability, then go to guest services when you first enter any theme park. Guest services will register your family member, take their photo, and provide the disability access service card.

After you have obtained the card go to a cast member at the front of the attraction your family would like to ride. The cast member will give you a time to return to enjoy the attraction by scanning everyone's MagicBand.

The time is determined by the current wait time. For example, if the wait time is one hour for Splash Mountain at 11am, you would receive a return time of 12 noon. When you return to the attraction everyone will go in the FastPass+ return line.

Chapter 7

Magic Kingdom attraction descriptions and recommendations for different age groups & tips

The Magic Kingdom

This chapter, along with the next three, will go into great detail about all attractions in Walt Disney World. The time lengths of the attractions will be shown too. This time was taken from when the attraction began and when it ended. It does not include pre-show time lengths.

Another feature of this chapter is a ratings score given for each attraction by my daughter Megan and my son Merino. The rating scale is from one to five with a five being the best ride ever and a one being an attraction they do not enjoy. Megan was thirteen years old at the time and a dare devil when it comes to thrill rides. She went on the Tower of Terror for the first time at age four. She loved the princesses when she was little, and enjoys the shows and attractions in Walt Disney World. My son Merino was nine years old and can be a bit more conservative. He has just started to enjoy the thrill rides at this age. He loved Buzz when he was little, loves the Star Wars attraction, and is definitely a fan of anything Disney.

Magic Kingdom attractions - Tomorrowland

Space Mountain: This is a must see attraction! You are seated behind one another in a six passenger rocket. Your rocket is on a roller coaster track that is indoors. On the ride you see stars, outer space, and experience unseen drops because it is very dark. FastPass+ is available, and the height requirement is 44". I highly recommend it if you and your family are thrill seekers. The wait time becomes very long as the morning and the day progresses. Try to go on early in the morning. If the standby line is outside the attraction, then try to get a FastPass+. FastPass+ will run out typically by the early evening. **Length of attraction:** 3 minutes 50 seconds. **Megan's rating: 5 & Merino's rating: 4.**

Space Mountain

Tomorrowland Speedway: It is a great family ride with a young child as you drive an Indy car that runs on a steel track. It can seat two people, but it does not go more than 10mph or so. During the day the wait is usually around 30 to 45 minutes. Your child has to be at least 32" and if they want to ride alone they have to be at least 54". FastPass+ is available, but I would not use one of your three early selections on this attraction. I still remember riding in the car with my children when they were very young. I let them drive and they had a blast! However, my body was thrown around as they kept slamming our car against the steel track. I still laughed the whole time! **Length of attraction:** 6 minutes 20 seconds. **Megan's rating: 4 & Merino's rating: 3.**

Tomorrowland Speedway

Astro Orbiter: This ride is similar to Dumbo. You fly in a rocket in a continuous circle. Two or four people can be in a rocket, and you can control it to go up and down. The wait can be long during the middle of the day. **Length of attraction:** 1 minute 30 seconds. **Megan's rating: 3 & Merino's rating: 2.**

Buzz Lightyear's Space Ranger Spin: Who wants to go to infinity and beyond? This is a fabulous attraction for Buzz Lightyear fans and the whole family. Two people ride in a slow moving vehicle. You shoot lasers at targets that have a "z" on them to score points. See if you can score 999,999. The wait is usually not that long but if it is, then you can get a FastPass+.

Length of attraction: 6 minutes 45 seconds. **Megan's rating: 3 & Merino's rating: 5.**

Stitch's Great Escape!: This attraction can be scary for young children. You are assisting in holding space criminals in a containment chamber. You sit in a dark chamber and Stitch will show up! The height requirement is 40". **Length of attraction:** 13 minutes 45 seconds. **Megan's rating: 3 & Merino's rating: 3.**

Tomorrowland Transit Authority PeopleMover: You ride in a slow moving vehicle to see all of Tomorrowland. The attraction is for everyone, and it is great to go on when you are waiting for a FastPass+ time for another attraction. **Length of attraction:** 11 minutes. **Megan's rating: 4 & Merino's rating: 4.**

Carousel of Progress: This show is a timeless classic. It was created by Walt Disney himself. You sit in a theater that actually moves through the history of the American family. Before you know it, you will be singing along to the catchy song in the show. It is the longest running stage show in the history of the American theater. There is never a wait for this attraction. **Length of attraction:** 21 minutes. **Megan's rating: 4 & Merino's rating: 4.**

Monster's Inc. Laugh Floor: A magnificent attraction that is very modern and interactive. The monsters have invited us, the humans, into their world. They tell jokes to the audience that you are seated in. The monsters interact with the audience too. Maybe you will get to be chosen as "That Guy!" It is fun for everyone and the wait is usually not longer than 20 minutes. **Length of attraction:** 13 minutes 45 seconds. FastPass+ is available. **Megan's rating: 5 & Merino's rating: 4.**

Monsters, Inc. Laugh Floor

Magic Kingdom attractions - Fantasyland

It's a Small World: Your party rides in a boat to see numerous different cultures around the world. Sing along with the continuous "It's a Small World" song. The wait is usually not ridiculous since a boat seats about 25 people. The kids might not be thrilled with this ride, but it is a classic original created by Walt himself. FastPass+ is available, but I would not use one of your three FastPass+ selections on it. **Length of attraction:** 12 minutes. **Megan's rating: 2 & Merino's rating: 1.**

Peter Pan's Flight: You will travel back to the movie "Peter Pan" and ride in a small ship that "flies" through different scenes from the movie. FastPass+ is available, and the standby line does get long quickly. Try to ride this in the morning if possible. **Length of attraction:** 3 minutes 15 seconds. **Megan's rating: 3 & Merino's rating: 3.**

Prince Charming Regal Carrousel: Ride one of Prince Charming's horses on this carousel. The wait is usually not that long, but the ride is over fairly quickly. So you know, Disney spells the ride this way. It is not an error. **Length of attraction:** 2 minutes. **Megan's rating: 2 & Merino's rating: 2.**

Princess Fairytale Hall: Your little princess can finally meet a real Disney princess at this meet and greet in the new Fantasyland! There are two different queues for this meet and greet. One is with Cinderella and Rapunzel and the other is with Anna and Elsa from the huge movie hit "Frozen." FastPass+ is available. If you want your child to meet Anna and Elsa, then obtain your FastPass+ 60 days before your trip! If you wait, you risk the chance of not obtaining a FastPass+. I have personally seen the standby wait time for this attraction reach 180 minutes! The meet and greet is located opposite the Carrousel.

Mickey's PhilharMagic: This is a definite must see attraction in the Magic Kingdom. You will experience unforgettable scenes from classic Disney movies and wonderful songs all Disney fans love. Beauty and the Beast and Aladdin are just two of the Disney movies represented. It is a 3D show that plays in a large theater. FastPass+ is available, but not necessary. If there is a wait, it will not be long, since the theater is very large. **Length of attraction:** 11 minutes 50 seconds. **Megan's rating: 4 & Merino's rating: 5.**

Mickey's PhilharMagic

The Many Adventures of Winnie the Pooh: A must see for all Pooh fans! You ride in a honey pot that seats four people at a time. You ride through the hundred acre wood and see Pooh and all his friends. FastPass+ is available and I would recommend it since the standby line can become very long by the afternoon. However, if you arrive before the Magic Kingdom opens, you will be able to go right through the standby line with little to no wait. **Length of attraction:** 3 minutes 30 seconds. **Megan's rating: 3 & Merino's rating: 5.**

Mad Tea Party: You will ride in a spinning tea cup that is under a circus tent. The tea cups usually seat four, and the more you turn the wheel, the faster your cup will spin. My son and daughter will attest to this, as they have tried to get me very sick! The line should go fairly fast. FastPass+ is available, but not necessary. Try to ride while waiting for a FastPass+ in Fantasyland. **Length of attraction:** 1 minute 30 seconds. **Megan's rating: 3 & Merino's rating: 3.**

Enchanted Tales with Belle: A truly magical attraction located in the new section of Fantasyland. I will not give away certain parts of the show, since it is something you must see to believe. You and your family will meet some of the characters from "Beauty and the Beast," and celebrate Belle's birthday with her. The kids can even be part of the show during this must see attraction!

FastPass+ is available. I recommend it since the standby time will become very long by the early afternoon. **Megan's rating: 5 & Merino's rating: 4.**

Under the Sea: Journey of the Little Mermaid: You get to ride in a clam and journey along into Ariel's world in this attraction. Your clam will take you through all the scenes from the movie "The Little Mermaid." You can sing along with all your favorite songs and witness some fabulous effects. FastPass+ is available and I would recommend reserving the FastPass+ for all the Ariel fans in your family. **Length of attraction:** 6 minutes 50 seconds. **Megan's rating: 4 & Merino's rating: 4.**

Under the Sea: Journey of the Little Mermaid

Ariel's Grotto: Your little girl or anyone in your family can have their picture taken with Ariel herself in this meet and greet location. Make sure to get there in time while she is still a mermaid. The lines will get long during the day and should be lighter at night. It is located on the same side as the "Under the Sea: Journey of the Little Mermaid" attraction. FastPass+ is available, but not necessary if you can arrive when the Magic Kingdom opens.

Seven Dwarfs Mine Train: This is the newest attraction in the Magic Kingdom. You embark on a journey into the world of the seven dwarfs. You ride in a train car that is a first of its kind ride system, since each train car will rock back and forth. The individual train cars are on a steel roller coaster track. The attraction is family friendly and you will hear music play as you enter the mine where a million diamonds shine. FastPass+ is available and the height requirement is 38". Typically the FastPass+ option will be gone about a month before your vacation. **Length of attraction:** 3 minutes 10 seconds. **Megan's rating: 3 & Merino's rating: 3.**

Seven Dwarfs Mine Train

Magic Kingdom attractions - Storybook Circus

Dumbo: This classic attraction is something that you should ride early in the morning. You ride in Dumbo himself, and two people ride at a time. The wait can get long late in the day, because only a small number of guests can ride the attraction at a time, however, FastPass+ is now available. **Length of attraction:** 1 minute 40 seconds. **Megan's rating: 2 & Merino's rating: 2.**

Dumbo

The Barnstormer featuring Goofy as the Great Goofini: Your small child will get to experience their first ever roller coaster! Take a ride with Goofy, and hang on tight! Two people can sit in a car, and you have to be at least 35". FastPass+ is available, but since the ride is only about thirty seconds long, I would not waist one of your initial three FastPass+ selections on it. **Megan's rating: 3 & Merino's rating: 4.**

Casey Jr. Splash 'N' Soak Station: This is a large play area for all the kids and kids at heart. Water is spraying everywhere, and you can try to shoot water at each other. There is no wait for the attraction since it is an open area. **Megan's rating: 3 & Merino's rating: 3.**

Pete's Silly Sideshow: This is a meet and greet with Goofy, Donald, Daisy, and Minnie. They are all dressed in circus outfits. After taking a picture with them, you will enter Big Top Treats and Souvenirs. You can get a tasty treat like cotton candy, caramel corn, and a character apple.

Magic Kingdom attractions - Frontierland

Splash Mountain: One word, "Yes!" Splash Mountain is a ton of fun and another must see attraction! Your party rides in a log that seats six into the world of Brer Rabbit and Brer Fox. There are many creative scenes and some celebratory music. There are a few small drops, and one large drop at the end. You must be at least 40" tall to ride, and the wait for the ride can become very long. I would recommend getting a FastPass+. **Length of attraction:** 11 minutes. **Megan's rating: 5 & Merino's rating: 5.**

Splash Mountain

Big Thunder Mountain Railroad: Come and ride a high speed train on a roller coaster track. It is a spectacular attraction if you like to move fast, and enjoy your heart pumping like a drummer pounding on a base drum. FastPass+ is available and everyone must be at least 40" to ride. Two people sit side by side in the train. The wait can get long by early in the afternoon. **Length of attraction:** 3 minutes 50 seconds. **Megan's rating: 5 & Merino's rating: 5.**

Big Thunder Mountain Railroad

Country Bear Jamboree: Come and watch the bears sing in this fun filled attraction for all the young ones in your family. Shows are continuous all day long, and the wait should be minimal. **Megan's rating: 2 & Merino's rating: 3.**

Tom Sawyer Island: You will take a boat over to explore Tom Sawyer Island. This is fun for the whole family, and there is not much of a wait at all to get over to the island. **Megan's rating: 1 & Merino's rating: 2.**

Magic Kingdom attractions - Liberty Square

The Hall of Presidents: This is a very intriguing attraction that will teach you some history, and wow you with moving figures of the United States Presidents. You sit in a very large theater, watch a video, and listen to the presidents speak. Shows run continuously throughout the day. It is air conditioned, and a great spot to take a rest and get out of the heat. Of course, this is more attractive for adults, and my wife and I enjoy it. My kids audibly groan when we say it's time for this attraction! **Length of attraction:** 20 minutes 40 seconds. **Megan's rating: 1 & Merino's rating: 2.**

The Hall of Presidents

Haunted Mansion: Are you ready for ghosts and scary rooms? This attraction is terrific! You ride in a slow moving "doom" buggy through the mansion. Music plays in your ears and the host of the mansion speaks to you. It is dark and some scenes are scary. Two people can ride in the buggy and possibly three if the third person is small. The wait time may get up to 45 minutes, but the line does move quickly. Walt Disney helped design this attraction. When your experience is over, see if a ghost will follow you home! FastPass+ is available, but not needed if you ride it in the morning or later at night. **Length of attraction:** 7 minutes 50 seconds. **Megan's rating: 3 & Merino's rating: 5.**

Haunted Mansion

Liberty Square Riverboat: When you need some down time head over to the Liberty Square Riverboat for a ride in a large boat down the river. The boat has plenty of seating and is constantly taking guests on tours. **Megan's rating: 3 & Merino's rating: 4.**

Magic Kingdom attractions - Adventureland

Swiss Family Treehouse: You and your party walk through the Robinson's home. There is never a wait and it will remind some adults of when they watched them on television years ago. **Megan's rating: 1 & Merino's rating: 1.**

Jungle Cruise: This is another attraction that was designed by Walt Disney. You ride in a boat through the many rivers of the world. Your tour guide is always entertaining and tells many funny little jokes. If there is a wait that is more than 30 minutes, guests have the option of getting a FastPass+. You could go on the Pirates of the Caribbean while waiting for your FastPass+ time. The first time my wife and I went on our tour guide yelled, "DUCK!" Everyone quickly ducked down thinking something was attacking the boat. Our tour guide gathered himself quickly and said calmly, "See there's a duck right there." Everyone, including myself, laughed at the goofy joke. **Length of attraction:** 9 minutes 40 seconds. **Megan's rating: 4 & Merino's rating: 3.**

The Magic Carpets of Aladdin: This attraction is very similar to Dumbo and Astro Orbiter. You sit in a magic carpet and go around and around. Your child can imagine they are with Aladdin and Jasmine. FastPass+ is available, but do not waste one of your three FastPass+ selections on it since the ride is over fairly quickly. The standby wait time will not get to the ridiculous level. **Length of attraction:** 1 minute 30 seconds. **Megan's rating: 2 & Merino's rating: 2.**

The Enchanted Tiki Room Under New Management: You sit in a large room and listen to the Tiki birds sing. Your family can sing along with them. There is typically no wait to go in the Enchanted Tiki Room, however, I have skipped it many times when visiting the Magic Kingdom. **Megan's rating: 1 & Merino's rating: 1.**

Pirates of the Caribbean: Grab your eye patch and climb aboard! The attraction inspired the Pirates of the Caribbean movies. Your party rides in a boat that seats approximately 30 people. You travel into the pirate world and will come face to face with Captain Jack Sparrow. The line moves fairly quickly because the boats seat a large number of people. FastPass+ is available for the attraction. **Length of attraction:** 10 minutes. **Megan's rating: 4 & Merino's rating: 4.**

Magic Kingdom attractions - Main Street, U.S.A.

Walt Disney World Railroad: Walt Disney loved trains, so he wanted one to circle his theme park. This railroad travels around the Magic Kingdom and stops in Frontierland, Storybook Circus, and Main Street, U.S.A. It is very large and seats numerous guests. Take a ride at some point during your day to experience the beauty of Walt's amazing theme park! **Length of attraction:** 20 minutes for all stops. **Megan's rating: 3 & Merino's rating: 4.**

Walt Disney World Railroad

Town Square Theater: Who wants to meet Mickey Mouse himself? Well, you can do it here! You enter the Town Square Theater to meet and have your picture taken with Mickey. FastPass+ is available, and the theater is located on the right after you enter the Magic Kingdom.

Tinker Bell in the Town Square Theater: If anyone in your family wants to meet Tinker Bell and her Fairy friends, then this is for you. This is not a ride, but you get to see Tinker Bell, her friends, and have your picture taken with them. It is also located in the Town Square Theater. It is not unusual to have a 30 minute wait. FastPass+ is now available for this meet and greet.

Tinker Bell meet and greet

Magic Kingdom Parades and Shows

Disney Festival of Fantasy Parade: Grab a seat along Main Street, U.S.A. or near Cinderella's Castle around 30 to 45 minutes before the parade starts to see all of your favorite characters. The characters will ride on floats in this magical parade. The characters will sing and dance with guests along the route. Make sure to wave to Mickey Mouse as he rides by. The parade is daily and usually starts at 3pm, but check your times guide for the exact time. FastPass+ is available, but get to the parade early and you will not have to use a FastPass+.

Disney Festival of Fantasy Parade

Dream Along with Mickey: This is a fabulous stage show directly in front of Cinderella's Castle. There are many characters that make an appearance, especially Mickey Mouse. There are show times throughout the day, so make sure to check your times guide for show times. **Length of show:** 20 minutes.

Move it! Shake it! Dance & Play it! Street Party: Your favorite Disney characters parade down Main Street, U.S.A. towards

Cinderella Castle. Mickey, Minnie, Donald, and Goofy will then be visible on giant gift boxes. They will encourage everyone to sing along with favorite party songs! Who is the best vocalist in your family?

Sorcerers of the Magic Kingdom: This is an interactive adventure throughout the Magic Kingdom. Merlin the Magician is going to make you a sorcerer's apprentice. You will cast spells as you find Merlin's other magic portals. You need to defend Mickey's park against the Disney villains.

A Pirate's Adventure: Treasure of the Seven Seas: This is an interactive adventure as you explore Adventureland to help Captain Jack Sparrow locate the Treasure of the Seven Seas. You will receive a pirate map and a magic talisman, which will assist you during your adventure. Look for a small building near the Pirates of the Caribbean, just past the arches, to get started.

A Pirate's Adventure

Main Street Electrical Parade: A must see night time parade! You will get to see all your favorite characters as they ride in floats covered with hundreds of twinkling lights that are synchronized to music. Sing along with all of your favorite songs and wave to Mickey and all of his friends! The parade does not occur every night. Check your times guide for the scheduled times. FastPass+ is available for the parade. However, if you want to see it, find a good spot 30 to 45 minutes before the parade. Then, you will be able to use your initial three FastPass+ selections elsewhere.

Wishes: This is one of the best firework shows on the planet! You and your family will watch incredible fireworks over the castle that is perfectly synchronized to Disney music. Some of the fireworks actually form into certain shapes. Wishes is nightly and usually begins at 9pm. Check your times guide for the exact time. FastPass+ is available, but again I would not recommend it. I would choose other attractions for FastPass+.

Wishes!

My Recommendations for the Magic Kingdom Attractions to see with young children ages 1-7

Take a picture in front of Cinderella's Castle.

Cinderella's Castle

Fantasyland

- It's a Small World ***FastPass+ available***
- Peter Pan's Flight ***FastPass+ available***
- Mickey's PhilharMagic ***FastPass+ available***
- Many Adventures of Winnie the Pooh ***FastPass+ available***
- Prince Charming Regal Carrousel
- Princess Fairytale Hall ***FastPass+ available***
- Mad Tea Party ***FastPass+ available***
- Seven Dwarfs Mine Train (38" to ride) ***FastPass+ available***
- Enchanted Tales with Belle ***FastPass+ available***
- Under the Sea: Journey of the Little Mermaid ***FastPass+ available***
- Ariel's Grotto ***FastPass+ available***

Storybook Circus

- Dumbo ***FastPass+ available***
- The Barnstormer featuring Goofy as the Great Goofini (35" to ride) ***FastPass+ available***
- Casey Jr. Splash 'N' Soak Station
- Pete's Silly Sideshow

Frontierland

- Country Bear Jamboree

- Splash Mountain (40" to ride) ***FastPass+ available***
- Big Thunder Mountain Railroad (40" to ride) ***FastPass+ available***
- Tom Sawyer Island

Liberty Square

- The Haunted Mansion (can be too scary for children) ***FastPass+ available***
- Liberty Square Riverboat

Adventureland

- The Magic Carpets of Aladdin ***FastPass+ available***
- Swiss Family Treehouse
- The Enchanted Tiki Room Under New Management
- Jungle Cruise ***FastPass+ available***
- Pirates of the Caribbean ***FastPass+ available***

Tomorrowland

- Space Mountain (44" to ride) ***FastPass+ available - use child swap* (Note: child swap is described in Chapter 12 under the Baby / Young Child tips)**
- Tomorrowland Speedway (32" to ride and 54" to ride alone) ***FastPass+ available***
- Tomorrowland Transit Authority PeopleMover
- Buzz Lightyear's Space Ranger Spin ***FastPass+**

available*

- Monsters, Inc. Laugh Floor ***FastPass+ available***
- Walt Disney's Carousel of Progress
- Astro Orbiter

Main Street, U.S.A.

- Walt Disney World Railroad
- Town Square Theater meet and greet with Mickey Mouse ***FastPass+ available***
- Tinker Bell in the Town Square Theater ***FastPass+ available***

Magic Kingdom parades and shows

- Disney Festival of Fantasy Parade ***FastPass+ available***
- Dream Along with Mickey
- Move it! Shake it! Dance & Play it! Street Party
- Main Street Electrical Parade ***FastPass+ available***
- Wishes ***FastPass+ available***

My Top 5 Must See Attractions in the Magic Kingdom for ages 1-7

1) Attractions in Storybook Circus
2) Monster's Inc. Laugh Floor
3) Mickey's PhilharMagic
4) Buzz Lightyear's Space Ranger Spin

5) Enchanted Tales with Belle

My Recommendations for the Magic Kingdom Attractions to see with children ages 8-12

Take a picture in front of Cinderella's Castle.

Tomorrowland

- Space Mountain (44" to ride) ***FastPass+ available***
- Tomorrowland Speedway (32" to ride and 54" to ride alone) ***FastPass+ available***
- Tomorrowland Transit Authority PeopleMover
- Buzz Lightyear's Space Ranger Spin ***FastPass+ available***
- Monsters, Inc. Laugh Floor ***FastPass+ available***
- Walt Disney's Carousel of Progress
- Astro Orbiter
- Stitch's Great Escape! (40" minimum)

Fantasyland

- It's a Small World ***FastPass+ available***
- Peter Pan's Flight ***FastPass+ available***
- Mickey's PhilharMagic ***FastPass+ available***
- Many Adventures of Winnie the Pooh ***FastPass+ available***
- Mad Tea Party ***FastPass+ available***

- Princess Fairytale Hall ***FastPass+ available***
- Seven Dwarfs Mine Train (38" to ride) ***FastPass+ available***

Seven Dwarfs Mine Train

- Enchanted Tales with Belle ***FastPass+ available***
- Under the Sea: Journey of the Little Mermaid ***FastPass+ available***
- Ariel's Grotto ***FastPass+ available***

Storybook Circus

- Dumbo ***FastPass+ available***
- The Barnstormer featuring Goofy as the Great Goofini (35" to ride) ***FastPass+ available***

- Casey Jr. Splash 'N' Soak Station
- Pete's Silly Sideshow

Frontierland

- Splash Mountain (40" to ride) ***FastPass+ available***
- Big Thunder Mountain Railroad (40" to ride) ***FastPass+ available***

Liberty Square

- The Haunted Mansion ***FastPass+ available***
- The Hall of Presidents

Adventureland

- The Magic Carpets of Aladdin ***FastPass+ available***
- Jungle Cruise ***FastPass+ available***
- Pirates of the Caribbean ***FastPass+ available***
- A Pirate's Adventure: Treasure of the Seven Seas

Main Street, U.S.A.

- Walt Disney World Railroad
- Town Square Theater ***FastPass+ available***
- Tinker Bell in the Town Square Theater ***FastPass+ available***

Magic Kingdom parades and shows

- Disney Festival of Fantasy Parade ***FastPass+ available***
- Dream Along with Mickey
- Sorcerers of the Magic Kingdom
- Move it! Shake it! Dance & Play it! Street Party
- Main Street Electrical Parade ***FastPass+ available***
- Wishes ***FastPass+ available***

My Top 5 Must See Attractions in the Magic Kingdom for ages 8-12

1) Space Mountain
2) Splash Mountain
3) Big Thunder Mountain Railroad
4) Seven Dwarfs Mine Train
5) Enchanted Tales with Belle

My Recommendations for the Magic Kingdom Attractions to see with children ages 13-17

Take a picture in front of Cinderella's Castle.

Tomorrowland

- Space Mountain (44" to ride) ***FastPass+ available***
- Tomorrowland Speedway (32" to ride and 54" to ride alone) ***FastPass+ available***
- Tomorrowland Transit Authority PeopleMover

- Buzz Lightyear's Space Ranger Spin ***FastPass+ available***
- Monsters, Inc. Laugh Floor ***FastPass+ available***
- Stitch's Great Escape! (40" minimum)
- Walt Disney's Carousel of Progress

Fantasyland

- It's a Small World ***FastPass+ available***
- Peter Pan's Flight ***FastPass+ available***
- Mickey's PhilharMagic ***FastPass+ available***
- Seven Dwarfs Mine Train (38" to ride) ***FastPass+ available***
- Princess Fairytale Hall ***FastPass+ available***
- Enchanted Tales with Belle ***FastPass+ available***
- Under the Sea: Journey of the Little Mermaid ***FastPass+ Available***

Storybook Circus

- Pete's Silly Sideshow

Liberty Square

- The Haunted Mansion ***FastPass+ available***
- The Hall of Presidents

Frontierland

- Splash Mountain (40" to ride) ***FastPass+ available***
- Big Thunder Mountain Railroad (40" to ride) ***FastPass+ available***

Adventureland

- Jungle Cruise ***FastPass+ available***
- Pirates of the Caribbean ***FastPass+ available***
- A Pirate's Adventure: Treasure of the Seven Seas

Main Street, U.S.A.

- Walt Disney World Railroad
- Town Square Theater ***FastPass+ available***

Meet Mickey Mouse

Magic Kingdom parades and shows

- Disney Festival of Fantasy Parade ***FastPass+ available***
- Dream Along with Mickey
- Move it! Shake it! Dance & Play it! Street Party
- Main Street Electrical Parade ***FastPass+ available***
- Wishes ***FastPass+ available***

My Top 5 Must See Attractions in the Magic Kingdom for ages 13-17

1) Space Mountain
2) Splash Mountain
3) Big Thunder Mountain Railroad
4) Seven Dwarfs Mine Train
5) Mickey's PhilharMagic

My Recommendations for the Magic Kingdom Attractions to see with adults only

Take a picture in front of Cinderella's Castle.

Tomorrowland

- Space Mountain (44" to ride) ***FastPass+ available***

Riding on Space Mountain

- Tomorrowland Transit Authority PeopleMover
- Buzz Lightyear's Space Ranger Spin ***FastPass+ available***
- Monsters, Inc. Laugh Floor ***FastPass+ available***
- Stitch's Great Escape! (40" minimum)
- Walt Disney's Carousel of Progress

Fantasyland

- It's a Small World ***FastPass+ available***
- Mickey's PhilharMagic ***FastPass+ available***

- Seven Dwarfs Mine Train (38" to ride) ***FastPass+ available***
- Enchanted Tales with Belle ***FastPass+ available***
- Under the Sea: Journey of the Little Mermaid ***FastPass+ available***

Storybook Circus

- Pete's Silly Sideshow

Liberty Square

- The Haunted Mansion ***FastPass+ available***
- The Hall of Presidents
- Liberty Square Riverboat

Frontierland

- Splash Mountain (40" to ride) ***FastPass+ available***
- Big Thunder Mountain Railroad (40" to ride) ***FastPass+ available***

Adventureland

- Jungle Cruise ***FastPass+ available***
- Pirates of the Caribbean ***FastPass+ available***

Main Street, U.S.A.

- Walt Disney World Railroad

- Town Square Theater ***FastPass+ available***

Looking down Main Street, U.S.A.

Magic Kingdom parades and shows

- Disney Festival of Fantasy Parade ***FastPass+ available***
- Dream Along with Mickey
- Move it! Shake it! Dance & Play it! Street Party
- Main Street Electrical Parade ***FastPass+ available***
- Wishes ***FastPass+ available***

My Top 5 Must See Attractions in the Magic Kingdom for adults only

1) Space Mountain
2) Splash Mountain
3) Big Thunder Mountain Railroad

4) The Haunted Mansion

5) Seven Dwarfs Mine Train

Magic Kingdom Tips

- Arrive 30 minutes before the park opens. You will want to see the opening ceremony. Mickey and his friends arrive on the Walt Disney World Railroad Train right in front of the park.
- Try the park entrance all the way to the left. It is for cast members and guests.
- Go to Space Mountain when you first arrive in the Magic Kingdom, if you have not already signed up for FastPass+.
- Try to make at least two of your FastPass+ selections for Space Mountain and the Seven Dwarfs Mine Train before your vacation. Then, enter the Magic Kingdom when it first opens and walk expeditiously over to Frontierland to ride Splash Mountain and Big Thunder Mountain. The attractions will have minimal waits for about the first hour after the park has opened.
- After you enter the Magic Kingdom in the morning and walk under the railroad, there will be characters in a large open circle area. You can take pictures with the characters and get autographs. Look for the ones that you are not dining with during your vacation.
- When you enter under the railroad look to the left. There

is a spot next to City Hall where a character will be located to take pictures and give autographs. It will usually be a character you do not see very often.

- If you have any questions, go into City Hall to guest relations, which is located on the left after you have entered the Magic Kingdom.
- The Harmony Barber Shop is a terrific place to get your child's haircut or your own. Haircuts are around $19 for adults and $18 for children. It is located on the left, just before you walk down Main Street. It is somewhat hidden in a side corner. You can make a reservation by calling (407) WDW-PLAY.
- Take a picture with Goofy on the bench in front of Tony's Town Square restaurant.
- A Starbucks, which was The Main Street Bakery, is a great place to grab a quick and easy breakfast. It is located on the right on Main Street. They have pastries, smoothies, croissant sandwiches, coffee, and numerous other choices.
- Look for the Mayor of Main Street to take a picture with him.
- When you are ready to have your picture taken with Mickey Mouse, make sure to enter the Town Square Theater. It is the least crowded early in the morning.
- If you are traveling with small children, go to Fantasyland early in the morning and ride Peter Pan. Then, experience

Dumbo in Storybook Circus. The crowds will be smaller here early on.

- While in the standby line for Winnie the Pooh look for the large glass window that seems to have honey flowing down from the top of it. Rub your hands in large circles on the glass and it will reveal hidden characters underneath. I would recommend using hand sanitizer afterwards due to the fact that thousands of people have rubbed the glass that day.
- At the end of your Seven Dwarfs Mine Train experience look to the right to see the Seven Dwarfs' house and you will see Snow White dancing. On the left side of the house you will see the evil witch too!
- Explore Belle's Village in the new section of Fantasyland. Your family will want to see the shops, especially Gaston's Tavern.
- Gaston's Tavern is an attraction in itself. There is music playing and antlers are everywhere. You can sit outside or inside and take a seat near the fireplace to view Gaston's portrait. Make sure to grab a snack, especially a warm cinnamon roll.
- Eat lunch at Be Our Guest Restaurant around 11am because the line will become very long at noon. The restaurant is a counter service location for lunch and you can make a dining reservation too.

- If you would like extra mayonnaise while eating lunch at Be Our Guest Restaurant, just ask at the soft drink area.
- There is a great photo spot near the castle to the right side of it. If you turn right towards Tomorrowland, look for a path on the left, and it goes near the castle. There is a wishing well where you can take a picture.
- There is a shortcut from Main Street to Tomorrowland and back to Main Street that goes through the Tomorrowland Terrace Restaurant. You can avoid huge crowds this way.
- You can beat the crowds on Main Street by going through the shops on the left or right.
- If you are planning to experience the day parade, get a spot somewhere on the parade route 30 to 45 minutes before it starts.
- While waiting in line at the Haunted Mansion, touch the instruments and the piano in the graveyard area. You will hear them play music.
- Before entering the Haunted Mansion, find the last gravestone on the left. The lady's eyes will open.
- When you get in the Haunted Mansion you will first enter one room and then another. While in the second room, stand under the woman holding an umbrella. The door behind you will open, and you will get ahead of the crowd to go on the ride.
- While in the Haunted Mansion, try to find the ghost who

is playing the piano.

- Notice that there is a 13 on the clock inside the Haunted Mansion.
- If you do not wish to see the day parade, it is a great time to hit some of the big rides, especially Splash Mountain or Pirates of the Caribbean. A large crowd will be attending the parade, so the wait times will be minimal.
- If you do not want to get soaked on Splash Mountain, then do not sit in the front seat. You may get wet in the other seats, but probably not soaked.

Splash Mountain seats

- There is a fun filled small playground for young children next to the Splash Mountain lines. Go down the stairs near the entrance, and you will find it on the right.

Splash Mountain play area

- There is a spot for a member of your family to take a picture of everyone riding Splash Mountain. They should stand on the bridge across from Pecos Bill's entrance sign. They will get a picture of the group just after they have gone down the huge drop.
- There is a walkway from Adventureland to Frontierland behind the Magic Carpets.
- There is a walkway from Frontierland to Adventureland next to the Country Bear Jamboree.
- While on the Buzz Lightyear ride, try to hit the "z" on the bottom of Zurg and on the top of the mountain. It will give you a surge of points.

Buzz perfect score!

- There are FastPass+ kiosks next to Stitch's Great Escape.
- There are FastPass+ kiosks in front of Mickey's PhilharMagic.
- There are FastPass+ kiosks next to the Jungle Cruise attraction.
- There are FastPass+ kiosks between the Diamond Horseshoe and the Frontier Trading Post.
- There is a shaded section near Buzz Lightyear Space Ranger Spin with some benches to sit on.
- To get out of the heat, go in the exit of Space Mountain, which does contain a gift shop.
- When waiting for a FastPass+ time in Tomorrowland, visit the Carousel of Progress, the Tomorrowland Transit Authority PeopleMover, or Monster, Inc. Laugh Floor.
- While in the Carousel of Progress, look on top of the

fireplace mantle during the last scene. The nutcracker on the far left is a Mickey Mouse.

- When you have a family member on the Tomorrowland Speedway, there is a grandstand viewing area to watch them race.
- Look for the talking trash can in Tomorrowland.
- There is a hidden walkway from Tomorrowland to Storybook Circus. If you exit Space Mountain, go to the extreme right. Follow the path and it will take you past the Barnstormer.

Walkway from Tomorrowland to Storybook Circus

- See the Flag Ceremony at 5pm at the United States flag on Main Street. The Pledge of Allegiance, Star Spangled

Banner, and God Bless America are performed.

Flag Ceremony

- You can join the dance party in Tomorrowland that is on the stage to the left of the Carousel of Progress. It occurs a few nights a week.

Magic Kingdom dance party in Tomorrowland

- After ordering your meal at Cosmic Ray's Starlight Cafe, look to eat in the dining room to hear Sonny Eclipse or eat on the patio to the right of Bay three.
- Look to get autographs and pictures with Woody and Jessie from "Toy Story" on the left after you exit Splash Mountain every 30 minutes or so.
- There is a walkway from the Haunted Mansion to Big Thunder Mountain and Splash Mountain. It will be key to use to avoid parade time crowds.

Walkway to Big Thunder Mountain and Splash Mountain

- Eat upstairs at the Columbia Harbour House. It is much quieter. After lunch or dinner, order the cobbler for dessert. It is delicious!
- Pecos Bill Tall Tale Inn and Cafe in Frontierland has an incredible topping bar.
- In Frontierland, there is a shaded area and bathrooms right near the Diamond Horseshoe.
- Visit the mobile food cart near the Jungle Cruise to grab a quick snack of a vegetable or cheeseburger egg roll.
- If you are going to one of the Hoop Dee Doo Musical Revue shows, you can take a boat from the resort launch

area just after you exit the Magic Kingdom.

Resort Launches

- Auntie Gravity's Galactic Goodies has refreshing soft ice cream and sundaes. It is located in Tomorrowland, around the corner from Stitch's Great Escape.
- To view the fireworks, there are many good viewing spots. You could stand behind the castle in Fantasyland, in front of Mickey's PhilharMagic, in front of the entrance of the Mad Tea Party, in front of Space Mountain in Tomorrowland, on the second level of the train station on Main Street, or somewhere near the front of the castle.
- To guarantee a fabulous view of the fireworks, you could make a reservation for the Wishes Fireworks Dessert Party. It is a dessert buffet at the Tomorrowland Terrace. Adults are $49 and children are $29. You can make a

reservation by calling (407) WDW-DINE because seating is limited.

- If you do not want to see the night parade or Wishes, most attractions standby wait times become 20 minutes or less. These attractions include: Haunted Mansion, Big Thunder Mountain, Buzz Lightyear, Space Mountain, Splash Mountain, and Small World.
- Visit the Confectionary on Main Street at the end of the day to buy some cookies, candy, fudge, and other treats.
- There is a walkway to Disney's Contemporary Resort and Bay Lake Tower from the Magic Kingdom.

Walkway to Disney's Contemporary Resort

Chapter 8 - Disney's Animal Kingdom attraction descriptions and recommendations for different age groups & tips

Disney's Animal Kingdom attractions - Discovery Island

It's Tough to be a Bug!: Is it a good idea to step on a bug? These bugs will prove it is a horrible idea! It's Tough to be a Bug was inspired by the movie with the same name. You sit in a large theater that is actually inside the Tree of Life. You wear 3D glasses and are transported into the bug world. The theater gets dark and there are a few scary moments for younger ones. You will get touched in the back through your seat and the theater will appear to fill with smoke at one point. Shows are continuous all day long and the wait should only be around 20 minutes or less. FastPass+ is available. **Length of attraction:** 9 minutes 30 seconds. **Megan's rating: 3 & Merino's rating: 4.**

It's Tough to be a Bug!

Adventurers Outpost: This is a meet and greet with Mickey and Minnie. The location is indoors and obviously air conditioned. FastPass+ is available, but I would not use one of your initial three FastPass+ selections for it.

Adventurers Outpost

Africa

Festival of the Lion King: This is a must see show that is located in Africa. You sit in an enclosed theater and experience a Broadway style show. The characters from "Lion King" come to life and sing all your favorite songs from the movie. This celebration is not just limited to singing. You will experience breath taking acrobatics and amazing dance performances. This show does not run continuously throughout the day. Please consult your park times guide for show times. FastPass+ is available. Although there is not a bad seat in the house, it is wise for you and your family to arrive 25 to 30 minutes before the show if you do not have a FastPass+. **Length of attraction:** 31 minutes 20 seconds. **Megan's rating: 4 & Merino's rating: 3.**

Festival of the Lion King

Kilimanjaro Safaris: Have you ever been on an African Safari? Well, here is your chance! You will ride in a large safari vehicle that takes you through the African Savannah where no cages will be found. This is a one of a kind attraction where the animals roam freely. You will enjoy the sites of elephants, lions, cheetahs, and many other wild animals during your safari. You might even have a giraffe or rhino walk right up to your vehicle, so have the camera ready! Your family could experience this attraction more than once during your vacation, since it can be different every time. FastPass+ is available, but if you go on early in the morning you should be able to get on right away. **Length of attraction:** 21 minutes. **Megan's rating: 5 & Merino's rating: 4.**

Giraffe on Kilimanjaro Safaris

Pangani Forest Exploration Trail: This walking tour is an ideal attraction to visit, especially if you are waiting for your FastPass+ time at Kilimanjaro Safaris. Since it is a walking tour, there is never a wait. You will encounter beautiful fish, exotic birds, enormous hippos, gorillas, and so much more. **Megan's rating: 3 & Merino's rating: 3.**

Gorilla on Pangani Exploration Trail

Rafiki's Planet Watch

Habitat Habit!: This tour is on an outdoor discovery trail, where you will see even more exotic animals, and learn how to share your backyard with them. **Megan's rating: 3 & Merino's rating: 3.**

Conservation Station: This interactive area has exhibits on animal training, food preparation, and veterinary care. You will be able to view live animals on camera and learn some more fascinating facts about their habitat. **Megan's rating: 3 & Merino's rating: 3.**

Affection Section: You are able to pet the animals in this section of Rafiki's Planet Watch. They are rare animals from all over the world. The featured animals are goats and sheep. **Megan's rating: 3 & Merino's rating: 3.**

Asia

Flights of Wonder: Birds are flying everywhere! This attraction is located in the Asia section of Animal Kingdom. You sit in a large theater and are entertained by an amazing show starring all types of exotic birds. They fly through the theater and perform some funny tricks. There are specific show times during the day, so check your times guide for the show you want to see! FastPass+ is available. **Length of attraction:** 25 minutes. **Megan's rating: 3 & Merino's rating: 3.**

Expedition Everest: If you love roller coasters and thrills, this is the attraction for you! You travel in a train on coaster tracks to come face to face with the Yeti, the guardian and protector of the Forbidden Mountain. The train does travel into dark areas, goes backwards, and has a few fast drops. FastPass+ is available, and you have to be at least 44" to ride. I would recommend selecting a FastPass+ time in advance for first thing in the morning and then go in the standby line. When you are done, your FastPass+ may be ready so you can go on again! This is my son's favorite attraction. **Length of attraction:** 4 minutes. **Megan's rating: 5 & Merino's rating: 5.**

Expedition Everest

Maharajah Jungle Trek: This is an impressive walking tour where you will experience even more amazing animals and have fun along the way. During your tour you get to see bats, birds, tigers, and many others. It is a great attraction to see while waiting for a FastPass+ time in Asia. **Megan's rating: 3 & Merino's rating: 4.**

Kali River Rapids: Experience whitewater rafting on this fun filled attraction! You and your party will sit in a large raft as you travel along the Chakranadi River. Be prepared, as with any whitewater rafting experience, you will get wet, soaked is more like it! FastPass+ is available and 38 inches is the height requirement. **Length of attraction:** 9 minutes 30 seconds. **Megan's rating: 4 & Merino's rating: 5.**

Kali River Rapids

Dinoland U.S.A

DINOSAUR: You will travel in a time rover back to the era of the dinosaurs in The Dino Institute. Your time rover will bounce, make quick turns, and you will experience some very dark times during this ride. Dinosaurs are everywhere and they may even attack the rover. It is a fun attraction, but it may be too scary for the little ones. The rover seats twelve, and you must be at least 40" to ride. FastPass+ is available, but if you go to Dinosaur in the morning the crowds will be light. **Length of attraction:** 4

minutes 30 seconds. **Megan's rating: 5 & Merino's rating: 5.**

Dinosaur skeleton inside DINOSAUR

Primeval Whirl: This attraction is incredible fun for all the coaster fans. It is not a traditional coaster. You ride in a single car that is round and not connected to other cars. Your coaster spins, goes around curves, and down hills. This attraction is outdoors, as opposed to most Walt Disney World attractions. It does have a height requirement of 48". As the day goes on, you will experience longer and longer wait times, so it's best to hit this attraction early in the day. FastPass+ is available. **Length of attraction:** 4 minutes. **Megan's rating: 4 & Merino's rating: 5.**

Riding on Primeval Whirl

Finding Nemo – The Musical: You experience a live performance using large puppets as the movie is transformed into a musical. Disney has created some fabulous music to go along with the scenes from the movie. This is not a continuous running attraction, so consult your times guide for show times. You will sit in a large theater, but do get to the show 30 minutes before it begins to ensure you get a seat. FastPass+ is available. **Length of attraction:** 40 minutes. **Megan's rating: 1 & Merino's rating: 1.**

Boneyard: This is a play area for kids and kids at heart! Kids can climb, go down slides, and will have a smile from ear to ear like

Pooh Bear does when he is eating a bowl full of honey. It is great to do if you are waiting for a FastPass+ time at Dinosaur. **Megan's rating: 4 & Merino's rating: 5.**

TriceraTop Spin: Have you ever wanted to ride in a dinosaur? It is possible with this attraction. It is very similar to Dumbo in the Magic Kingdom. You can take your child in a flying TriceraTop. You will go around in a circle, nice and slow, and you have the option of making your TriceraTop go up or down. The wait is typically only around 20 minutes. **Length of attraction:** 1 minute 45 seconds. **Megan's rating: 3 & Merino's rating: 3.**

My Recommendations for Disney's Animal Kingdom attractions to see with young children ages 1-7

Take a picture in front of the Tree of Life.

Tree of Life

Africa

- Kilimanjaro Safaris ***FastPass+ available***
- Festival of the Lion King (**see times guide for show times) *FastPass+ available***
- Pangani Forest Exploration Trail

Asia

- Expedition Everest (44" to ride) ***FastPass+ available - use child swap***
- Maharajah Jungle Trek
- Kali River Rapids (38" to ride) ***FastPass+ available***
- Flights of Wonder (**see times guide for show times) *FastPass+ available***

Dinoland U.S.A.

- TriceraTop Spin
- Finding Nemo - The Musical (**see times guide for show times**) ***FastPass+ available***
- The Boneyard
- Dinosaur (40" to ride) ***FastPass+ available - use child swap***
- Primeval Whirl (48" to ride) ***FastPass+ available***

Discovery Island

- Discovery Island Trails (walk around the Tree of Life to

see it up close)

- Adventurers Outpost ***FastPass+ available***

Rafiki's Planet Watch

- Wildlife Express Train (Train to attractions)
- Habitat Habit!
- Conservation Station
- Affection Section

My Top 5 Must See Attractions in Disney's Animal Kingdom for ages 1-7

1) Festival of the Lion King
2) The Boneyard
3) Kilimanjaro Safaris
4) Finding Nemo - The Musical
5) Maharajah Jungle Trek

My Recommendations for Disney's Animal Kingdom attractions to see with children ages 8-12

Take a picture in front of the Tree of Life.

Africa

- Kilimanjaro Safaris ***FastPass+ available***

Lion in Kilimanjaro Safaris

- Festival of the Lion King (**see times guide for show times) *FastPass+ available***
- Pangani Forest Exploration Trail

Asia

- Expedition Everest (44" to ride) ***FastPass+ available***

Riding on Expedition Everest

- Maharajah Jungle Trek
- Kali River Rapids (38" to ride) ***FastPass+ available***
- Flights of Wonder (**see times guide for show times**) ***FastPass+ available***

Dinoland U.S.A.

- Dinosaur (40" to ride) ***FastPass+ available***
- Primeval Whirl (48" to ride) ***FastPass+ available***
- Finding Nemo - The Musical (**see times guide for show times**) ***FastPass+ available***
- The Boneyard

Discovery Island

- Discovery Island Trails (walk around the Tree of Life to see it up close)
- It's Tough to be a Bug ***FastPass+ available***
- Adventurers Outpost ***FastPass+ available***

Rafiki's Planet Watch

- Wildlife Express Train (Train to attractions)
- Habitat Habit!
- Conservation Station
- Affection Section

My Top 5 Must See Attractions in Disney's Animal Kingdom for ages 8-12

1) Expedition Everest
2) Festival of the Lion King
3) Dinosaur
4) Kilimanjaro Safaris
5) Primeval Whirl

My Recommendations for Disney's Animal Kingdom attractions to see with children ages 13-17 & adults only

Take a picture in front of the Tree of Life.

Disney's Animal Kingdom entrance sign

Africa

- Kilimanjaro Safaris ***FastPass+ available***
- Festival of the Lion King (**see times guide for show times) *FastPass+ available***
- Pangani Forest Exploration Trail

Asia

- Expedition Everest (44" to ride) ***FastPass+ available***
- Maharajah Jungle Trek
- Kali River Rapids (38" to ride) ***FastPass+ available***
- Flights of Wonder (**see times guide for show times**) ***FastPass+ available***

Dinoland U.S.A.

- Dinosaur (40" to ride) ***FastPass+ available***
- Primeval Whirl (48" to ride) ***FastPass+ available***

Discovery Island

- Discovery Island Trails (walk around the Tree of Life to see it up close)
- It's Tough to be a Bug ***FastPass+ available***
- Adventurers Outpost ***FastPass+ available***

Rafiki's Planet Watch

- Wildlife Express Train (Train to attractions)
- Habitat Habit!
- Conservation Station
- Affection Section

<u>My Top 5 Must See Attractions in Disney's Animal Kingdom for ages 13-17 & adults only</u>

1) Expedition Everest
2) Festival of the Lion King
3) Dinosaur
4) Kilimanjaro Safaris
5) Primeval Whirl

<u>Animal Kingdom Tips</u>

- If you have a FastPass+ for Expedition Everest, then go over to the attraction when the park first opens and go in the standby line. The line will have no wait very early in the morning. After you ride, your FastPass+ may be ready.

- When on Expedition Everest, after you go backwards and then down two hills into a tunnel, look up to hopefully catch a glimpse of the Yeti.

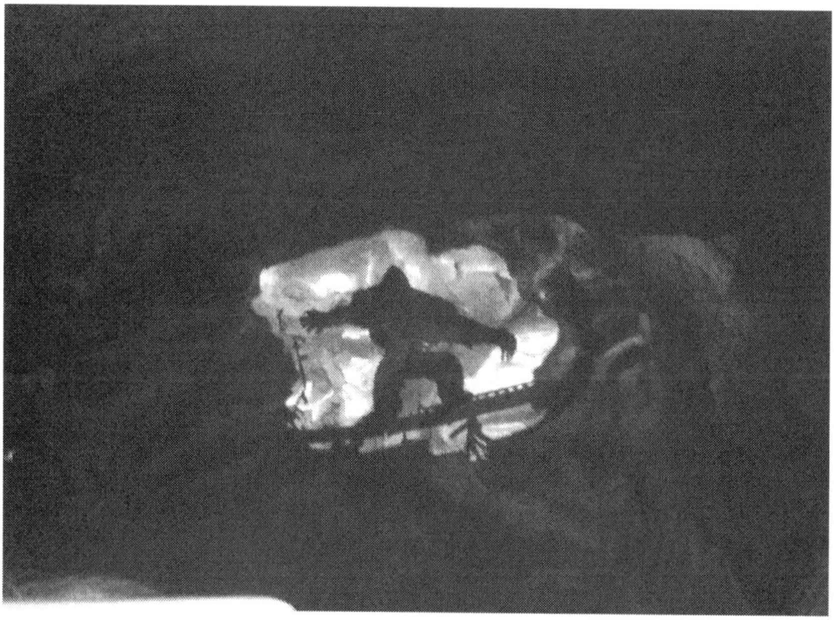

First Glimpse of the Yeti

- If you are a thrill seeker, then ask a cast member to seat you in the front on Expedition Everest.
- Try to experience Kilimanjaro Safaris in the early morning because the animals are more active.

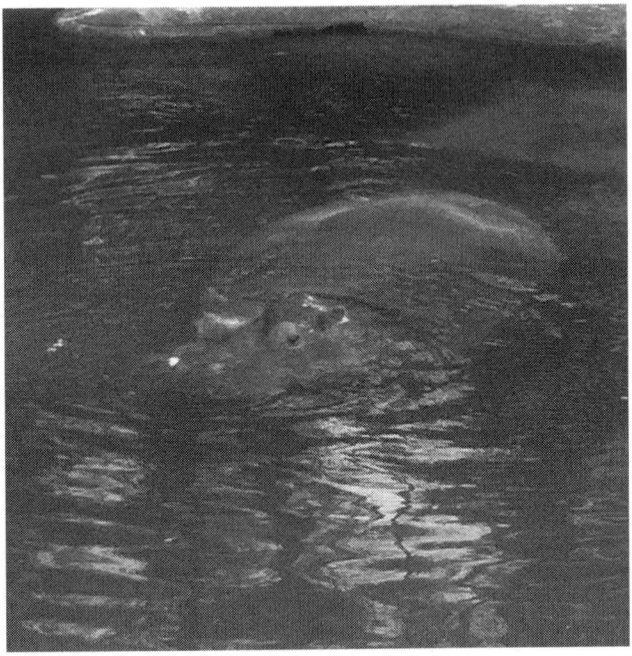

Hippo in Kilimanjaro Safaris

- If you have a stroller and are going on Kilimanjaro Safaris, you can stroll it up halfway through the line and a cast member will park it for you on the right.
- When you enter the vehicle for Kilimanjaro Safaris, make sure to sit on the outside of a row. It is the best place to take pictures of the animals.
- Dinoland is usually empty before 10am.
- There is a walkway from Africa to Asia. While on this walkway there will be a terrific spot for a photo with the Tree of Life in the background.
- There is a walkway from Asia to Dinoland U.S.A. The

easiest way to find it is to exit Expedition Everest and turn left. Follow the path past Finding Nemo and it will take you to Dinoland.

- While walking in Animal Kingdom, keep your eyes on the look-out for any animals near the walking paths.
- While in Africa, greet the cast members with the word "Jambo." It means "hello" in Swahili.
- Check out the Harambe Market in Africa.

Harambe Market

- The Festival of the Lion King is a must see. Check the times guide and make sure you get to a show.
- The cast members will begin to seat you 15 minutes before a Festival of the Lion King show.
- When you enter The Festival of the Lion King, do not sit

in the small seating area on the immediate right. The cast members allow guests to walk in front of that section if they need to leave the show early.

- Look at all the animals carved into the Tree of Life while you are walking in line to see It's Tough to be a Bug.
- At the very beginning of It's Tough to be a Bug, look up at the front of the theater to see "Flik."
- Visit the meet and greet with Mickey and Minnie called Adventurers Outpost in Discovery Island. FastPass+ is available.
- If you are a Starbucks fan then visit Creature Comforts. It is now a Starbucks location.

Creature Comforts

- If you have young children, make sure you visit the Boneyard in Dinoland U.S.A. It is a wonderful play area with slides, tubes, and ropes to climb.

- Dinosaur is a great attraction. However, it may be scary for some children because it is very dark with loud noises.
- In the attraction Dinosaur, have your camera ready to take a picture of the dinosaur skeleton just before the pre-show.
- Dinosaur has a shaded area to relax and have a seat when you need it, especially if you are waiting for your party that just went on the ride. If you are looking at the exit, it is on the left.
- Dino-Bite Snacks has some refreshing ice cream treats, muffins, and baked goods in Dinoland U.S.A.
- While in Dinoland U.S.A., look for the live American Crocodile near Dino-Bite Snacks.
- Trilo-Bites is located right after the bridge as you enter Dinoland U.S.A. They have waffles, milk shakes, floats, soda, and Bud Light.
- You may get soaked on Kali River Rapids.
- On Kali River Rapids, store your personal items that you want to remain dry in a large round compartment in the middle of your raft.
- There is an observation bridge for Kali River Rapids. A member of your party that does not want to experience the attraction can see everyone at one point.
- While on the observation bridge for Kali River Rapids, you can spray water on unaware guests by pressing a

button.

- If a new parade is created, the wait times for Expedition Everest, Dinosaur, and Kilimanjaro Safaris will drop about fifteen minutes before the parade begins.

Expedition Everest

- As you are walking to Expedition Everest from Africa, look over to the left and up. You will see wooden platforms with Asian monkeys on them. The monkeys are called Siamang.
- Have your child become a Wilderness Explorer by getting a Wilderness Explorers handbook. They will visit different areas of Disney's Animal Kingdom and earn badges by learning about animal nutrition and habitats,

just to name a few. Look for the symbol pictured here to get involved in the fun!

Wilderness Explorer

- When you exit It's Tough to be a Bug, you can turn left to go directly into Asia.
- There is a great snack deal of Lobster Mac & Cheese at a food stand just before you enter Asia. It is only one snack credit from the dining plan.

Lobster Mac & Cheese

- There are two FastPass+ kiosks across from each other on the path to the Tree of Life.
- There is a FastPass+ kiosk next to Kali River Rapids in Asia.
- There is a FastPass+ kiosk on the path to the Harambe Market in Africa.

Chapter 9

Disney's Hollywood Studios attraction descriptions and recommendations for different age groups & tips

Disney's Hollywood Studios attractions

Beauty and the Beast – Live on Stage: This is an extravagant Broadway style play of the classic Disney movie, "Beauty and the Beast." The acting and singing are just terrific. The show takes place in a very large theater that is near the Tower of Terror. FastPass+ is available and there are show times throughout the day. You need to grab a times guide to check on show times that fit into your schedule. I would recommend getting to the show 20 minutes early to get a good seat. I can still visualize my daughter, at 16 months old, cheering and clapping along with the music! **Length of attraction:** 25 minutes. **Megan's rating: 4 & Merino's rating: 2.**

Gaston from Beauty and the Beast

Disney Junior – Live on Stage: Your child will want to sing along with all of their favorite friends from Mickey Mouse Clubhouse, Winnie the Pooh, Handy Manny, and more. The characters are puppets on the stage and all the children can sing and jump along with the characters. Be aware that you will have to sit on a carpeted floor. There is limited bench seating for those that may have difficulty. There are show times throughout the day, so check your times guide for a show time. FastPass+ is also available. **Length of attraction:** 24 minutes. **Megan's rating: 2 & Merino's rating: 5.**

Disney Junior Live on Stage

For the First Time in Forever: A Frozen Sing-Along Celebration: You and your family will be able to join Anna and Elsa in this spectacular sing-along. It is in the Premiere Theater behind the Muppets attraction. The attraction has select show times throughout the day so check your times guide. The ending of the show features the hit song "Let It Go." Please note that there is no opportunity to meet the characters here. FastPass+ is available. **Length of attraction:** 30 minutes.

The Great Movie Ride: This is one of the original attractions in the Hollywood Studios. You and your family will ride in a large vehicle that seats about 60 guests. You travel through such movie classics as: Alien, Wizard of Oz, Casablanca, Tarzan, and many more. The attraction is a great experience and has some memorable movie clips at the end. FastPass+ is available, but not completely necessary. Even if the standby time is long, you will be entertained as you wait by movie previews in a large theater style area. The Great Movie Ride is straight ahead after you have entered the theme park. **Length of attraction:** 20 minutes. **Megan's rating: 4 & Merino's rating: 5.**

The Great Movie Ride

Honey, I Shrunk the Kids Movie Set Adventure: The attraction is a huge playground area that is similar to the movie "Honey, I Shrunk the Kids." Children can play on slides shaped like leaves and get some energy out as they run around. If you do not have little ones, then you can skip the area. **Megan's rating: 1 & Merino's rating: 3.** (This attraction is closing in 2016.)

Indiana Jones Epic Stunt Spectacular: A must see for any Indiana Jones fan! Witness a live stunt show and see how Indiana does his amazing stunts. You will see a few different scenes from the movies, and the sets will change right before your eyes. You even have the chance to be chosen as an extra. Jump around like Goofy and they may pick you! There are show times throughout the day. Check your times guide for the show you want to see. It is recommended you arrive about 30 minutes before the start of the show, if you do not have a FastPass+. **Length of attraction:** 31 minutes 15 seconds. **Megan's rating: 5 & Merino's rating: 5.**

Jedi Training Academy: Grab your light saber of choice and get ready! Your child will be on stage and learn from a real Jedi. Darth Vader himself will make an appearance to take on all the young Jedis. This is a show you have to sign up for first thing in the morning. Your child must be ages 4 - 12 and must be present when you sign up. To register, go to the "ABC Sound Studio" and look for a sign out front. The shows will fill up by the early morning. There are only a certain amount of shows per day, so check your times guide. **Megan's rating: 2 & Merino's rating: 5.**

Darth Vader

Lights, Motors, Action! Extreme Stunt Show: This is a high energy stunt show with cars and motorcycles. You will learn how big movie stunts are done and how everyone is kept safe. Two shows usually take place every day, and the shows are around 35 minutes long. I would recommend getting to the show 20 minutes early to be sure you get a seat or get a FastPass+. **Megan's rating: 3 & Merino's rating: 4.** (This attraction is closing in 2016.)

Muppet Vision 3D: You will be entertained the entire time during this throwback show! You start off by entering a pre-show area. The Muppets will make you laugh with their funny antics. The main show is in a large theater, where Kermit and friends are trying to create 3D. The show will remind you of your days as a kid watching The Muppet Show. Shows are continuous all day long and even if there is a wait, the pre-show makes it seem like no wait at all. However, you do have the option of making it a FastPass+ selection, but I do not think FastPass+ is necessary. **Length of attraction:** 14 minutes 45 seconds. **Megan's rating: 3 & Merino's rating: 5.**

Muppet Vision 3D

Rock 'n' Roller Coaster Starring Aerosmith: Go from 0 to 60 miles per hour in 2.8 seconds! Yes, when you ride the indoor Rock 'n' Roller Coaster you will take off in your roller coaster from a dead stop and rocket up to 60mph. It is a real rush as you go through loops and some California icons, all while listening to Aerosmith music. The height requirement is 48". FastPass+ is available, and I highly recommend it because wait times get long very early in the day. Another option is the single rider line. If your family chooses this line, you will not ride together. **Length of attraction:** 2 minutes 45 seconds. **Megan's rating: 5 & Merino's rating: 5.**

Rock 'n' Roller Coaster Starring Aerosmith

Star Tours: A must see for all Star Wars fans! You ride in a flight simulator that is in stunning 3D. You are taking a ship to another planet that is attacked by the Empire. Your flight goes through a number of possible scenes and the experience can be different each time you ride. You may be chosen as the rebel spy! The height requirement is 40". FastPass+ is available, but is usually not needed in the early morning hours. **Length of attraction:** 5 minutes. **Megan's rating: 3 & Merino's rating: 5.**

Outside of Star Tours

Star Wars Launch Bay: The new generation of the force and Star Wars has arrived in the Hollywood Studios! As you enter the launch bay you will enter the Launch Bay Theater and hear from the creators of the newest Star Wars trilogy. Next, you will encounter all types of movie memorabilia, the Star Wars cantina, and have the chance to meet Chewbacca and Darth Vadar. **Merino's rating: 5.**

Star Wars Launch Bay

Toy Story Midway Mania!: An absolute must see attraction for the entire family. You will sit in a vehicle that seats four and play midway style games that are similar to being at a state fair. These games include: ring toss, popping balloons, and breaking plates. You play these games in a 4D style format using a pull gun that shoots into a screen. See if you can beat the high score for the day! FastPass+ is available, and I highly recommend signing up for one before your vacation. **The FASTPASSES can be gone 40 days in advance.** **Length of attraction:** 6 minutes 30 seconds. **Megan's rating: 4 & Merino's rating: 5.**

The Twilight Zone Tower of Terror: As my daughter Megan would say, "My body is shaking! That was so awesome!" You check into the Hollywood Hotel and ride one of the most thrilling attractions in Walt Disney World and on the planet. The pre-show sets the mood as you see that former guests of the hotel traveled into the twilight zone. You will ride an elevator that has multiple drops of 13 stories that can be different all the time. There is a height requirement of at least 40 inches, and it will be scary for little ones. FastPass+ is available and as the day goes on, the wait in the standby line will get longer and longer. I highly recommend obtaining a FastPass+ for this ride. It's a family favorite. You will not be disappointed, but you may disappear! **Length of attraction:** 3 minutes 15 seconds. **Megan's rating: 5 & Merino's rating: 4.**

Tower of Terror elevator

Voyage of the Little Mermaid: Your family will join Ariel and friends under the sea in this impressive theatrical production. You will see and hear Ariel herself sing on stage as well as Flounder and Ursula. The shows run continuously and the entire family is sure to love it. FastPass+ is available, but not necessary. **Length of attraction:** 15 minutes 50 seconds. **Megan's rating: 3 & Merino's rating: 1.**

Voyage of the Little Mermaid

Walt Disney: One Man's Dream: Everyone in your family should visit this attraction to honor the man who had the vision to create Walt Disney World, and learn about his history. At the end of the museum is a fifteen minute video about Walt's life that I believe is a must see. This is a great attraction to experience when your family is waiting for a FastPass+ time, or you need to get indoors. **Megan's rating: 3 & Merino's rating: 5.**

Hollywood Studios Parades and Shows

Fantasmic!: An absolute must see in Walt Disney World! The words I am writing do not even do this night time show justice. Mickey will fight the Disney villains, including a dragon, while he extinguishes a lake that actually lights on fire. All the characters make an appearance in the show. The theater is outdoors, and it fills to capacity quickly. The show does not occur every night, so check your times guide. Arrive in line an hour or more before the start of the show to get a seat. FastPass+ is available, but I would not use one on Fantasmic. The reason being you can only make three initial FastPass+ selections. If this is one of them, then you will not be able to get a 4th FastPass+ later in the day because the show does not begin until at least 7pm or later. You can take advantage of the Fantasmic Dining Package. **Make sure to refer back to chapter four for information on this dining package.**

Fantasmic!

My Recommendations for Disney's Hollywood Studios attractions to see with young children ages 1-7

Disney's Hollywood Studios sign

- Toy Story Midway Mania! ***FastPass+ available***
- Muppet Vision 3-D ***FastPass+ available***
- For the First Time in Forever: A Frozen Sing-Along Celebration ***FastPass+ available* *check for show times***
- Honey, I Shrunk the Kids Movie Set Adventure
- The Great Movie Ride ***FastPass+ available***
- Voyage of the Little Mermaid ***FastPass+ available***

Ariel singing in Voyage of the Little Mermaid

- Disney Junior - Live on Stage! ***FastPass+ available*** ***check for show times***
- Star Wars Launch Bay
- Star Tours (40" to ride) ***FastPass+ available***
- Jedi Training Academy (located to the left of Star Tours) ***check for show times***
- Indiana Jones Epic Stunt Spectacular! ***FastPass+ available*** ***check for show times***

Indiana Jones Epic Stunt Spectacular

- Lights, Motors, Action! Extreme Stunt Show ***FastPass+ available* *check for show times***
- The Twilight Zone Tower of Terror (40" to ride) ***FastPass+ available - use child swap***
- Beauty and the Beast-Live on Stage ***FastPass+ available* *check for show times***
- Rock 'n' Roller Coaster Starring Aerosmith (48" to ride) ***FastPass+ available - use child swap***

Hollywood Studios Parades and Shows

- Fantasmic! ***FastPass+ available***

My Top 5 Must See Attractions in Disney's Hollywood Studios for Girls ages 1-7

1) Voyage of the Little Mermaid

2) Beauty and the Beast-Live on Stage!

3) Disney Junior - Live on Stage!

4) Muppet Vision 3-D

5) Toy Story Midway Mania!

My Top 5 Must See Attractions in Disney's Hollywood Studios for Boys ages 1-7

1) Toy Story Midway Mania!

2) Star Wars Launch Bay

3) Disney Junior - Live on Stage!

4) Muppet Vision 3-D

5) Indiana Jones Epic Stunt Spectacular!

My Recommendations for Disney's Hollywood Studios attractions to see with children ages 8-12

- The Twilight Zone Tower of Terror (40" to ride) ***FastPass+ available***

Tower of Terror

- Rock 'n' Roller Coaster Starring Aerosmith (48" to ride) ***FastPass+ available***
- Beauty and the Beast-Live on Stage ***FastPass+ available* *check for show times***
- Toy Story Midway Mania! ***FastPass+ available***
- Muppet Vision 3-D ***FastPass+ available***
- For the First Time in Forever: A Frozen Sing-Along Celebration ***FastPass+ available* *check for show times***
- Honey, I Shrunk the Kids Movie Set Adventure

- The Great Movie Ride ***FastPass+ available***

Inside the Great Movie Ride

- Voyage of the Little Mermaid ***FastPass+ available***
- Star Wars Launch Bay
- Star Tours (40" to ride) ***FastPass+ available***
- Jedi Training Academy (located to the left of Star Tours) ***check for show times***
- Indiana Jones Epic Stunt Spectacular! ***FastPass+ available* *check for show times***
- Lights, Motors, Action! Extreme Stunt Show ***FastPass+ available* *check for show times***
- Walt Disney: One Man's Dream

Hollywood Studios Parades and Shows

- Fantasmic! ***FastPass+ available***

My Top 5 Must See Attractions in Disney's Hollywood Studios for ages 8-12

1) The Twilight Zone Tower of Terror

2) Rock 'n' Roller Coaster Starring Aerosmith

3) Toy Story Midway Mania!

4) Star Tours

5) Beauty and the Beast-Live on Stage

My Recommendations for Disney's Hollywood Studios attractions to see with children ages 13-17 & adults only

- The Twilight Zone Tower of Terror (40" to ride) ***FastPass+ available***
- Rock 'n' Roller Coaster Starring Aerosmith (48" to ride) ***FastPass+ available***

Rock 'n' Roller Coaster about to begin!

- Beauty and the Beast-Live on Stage ***FastPass+ available* *check for show times***
- Toy Story Midway Mania! ***FastPass+ available***
- Muppet Vision 3-D ***FastPass+ available***
- The Great Movie Ride ***FastPass+ available***
- Voyage of the Little Mermaid ***FastPass+ available***
- Star Wars Launch Bay
- Star Tours (40" to ride) ***FastPass+ available***
- Indiana Jones Epic Stunt Spectacular! ***FastPass+ available* *check for show times***

- Lights, Motors, Action! Extreme Stunt Show ***FastPass+ available* *check for show times***
- Walt Disney: One Man's Dream

Hollywood Studios Parades and Shows

- Fantasmic! ***FastPass+ available***

My Top 5 Must See Attractions in Disney's Hollywood Studios for ages 13-17 & adults only

1) The Twilight Zone Tower of Terror
2) Rock 'n' Roller Coaster Starring Aerosmith
3) Toy Story Midway Mania!
4) Star Tours
5) Beauty and the Beast – Live on Stage

Hollywood Studios Tips

- Before your vacation, make sure you sign up for a FastPass+ online for Toy Story Midway Mania. FastPass+ times will be gone for the attraction about 40 days in advance.
- The FastPass+ line for Toy Story Midway Mania may be on the same side as the attraction Walt Disney: One Man's Dream early in the morning.
- Toy Story is a must see attraction for the whole family.

Toy Story Midway Mania!

- Arrive at the theme park 30 minutes before the park official opens. If you have a FastPass+ for Toy Story, then walk over to the Rock 'n' Roller Coaster when you enter the park. The standby line will have a very short wait. After you ride, walk to the Tower of Terror and the standby line will be minimal too. You should be able to ride the Tower of Terror multiple times early in the morning.
- If you want to have your child participate in the Jedi Training Academy, then arrive 30 minutes before the park opens. When you get inside the park, an adult in your family has to bring your child directly to the Jedi Training Academy to sign up.
- Try to ride Star Tours a few times. There are actually 54 different combinations of the ride program.

Star Tours

- If you like Star Wars, look into watching the Jedi Training Academy show. Check your times guide for show times.
- Tatooine Traders is the Star Tours gift shop. You can buy numerous items for the Star Wars fan in your family. You can enter the shop without even experiencing the attraction. It is to the right of the Star Tours entrance.

Tatooine Traders

- Starring Rolls Café is a great place to get a quick breakfast after riding the Tower of Terror or Rock 'n' Roller Coaster Starring Aerosmith. It has a relaxing area outside to sit down.

Starring Rolls Café

- A location serving Starbucks coffee and pastries has opened. It is called the Trolley Car Café.
- If anyone in your family is into Toy Story, make sure you visit the Pizza Planet Arcade for lunch or to play a game. There is plenty of seating in the upstairs area.
- Try to avoid eating at Rosie's or Catalina Eddie's right after a Beauty and the Beast show has ended. There will usually be large lines at those times.
- When you enter the pre-show for the Twilight Zone Tower of Terror, move to the back side of the library on the

opposite side of the TV. You will be right next to the door that will open, and you will get ahead of everyone else.

- During the pre-show video and the video while riding the Tower of Terror, look for the little girl. You will notice that she is holding a small stuffed animal Mickey Mouse.
- When the elevator moves forward in the Tower of Terror look to the right and you will see a picture of everyone in the elevator.
- If your family goes on the Tower of Terror, and you decide not to partake in the excitement, go to the right of the Tower of Terror and enter the gift shop. Walk to the back of the gift shop and there are benches with cushions to sit on while you wait for your family. After they ride, they will enter the gift shop and will find you there.
- Grab a coffee or a pastry at the exit of the Tower of Terror.
- Avoid the Tower of Terror and Rock 'n' Roller Coaster standby lines right after a Beauty and the Beast show has ended.
- There are bathrooms located on the right before the Tower of Terror.
- After you walk under the upside down limo coaster for the Rock ‘n’ Roller Coaster, go to the left and you will find an area to sit, get some shade, get a drink at the water fountains, or use the bathroom.
- If you are a thrill seeker, ask to sit in the front row at the

Rock 'n' Roller Coaster.

- Your family will enjoy the street performers called the Citizens of Hollywood. They perform on Sunset Blvd. in front of the Beverly Sunset Sweet Spells, which is on the street to the Tower of Terror.

Citizens of Hollywood

- On Hollywood Boulevard be on the lookout for a vehicle that says "Hollywood Public Works." The actors in the vehicle perform entertaining shows throughout the day.

Hollywood Public Works vehicle

- When the new parade begins again, there is great seating for the parade on the steps in front of the former American Idol attraction. It is shaded, and the parade route is scheduled to pass in front of that area. Try to get there 30 minutes before the parade starts. The parade usually begins at 3pm, but check your times guide to be sure.
- Min and Bill's Dockside Diner has refreshing vanilla and chocolate shakes.
- If you go to Disney Junior, be aware that there are no seats. Everyone sits on the floor. There are only a few benches against the wall.
- Get to the Lights, Motors, Action! Extreme Stunt Show 30 minutes early. It usually only runs twice daily.

- Meet characters from the movie “Cars” on Streets of America in front of Luigi’s garage.
- While riding the attraction The Great Movie Ride, look for John Wayne and Clint Eastwood. Make sure to also look for the witch of the East's legs in the Wizard of Oz scene. Her legs are in the very beginning on the right, under a house.
- Before experiencing the Great Movie ride make sure you calculate if you have enough time so you will not miss an upcoming FastPass+. The attraction is 25 minutes in length.
- There is a FastPass+ kiosk on the corner of Hollywood Boulevard and Sunset Boulevard.
- There is a FastPass+ kiosk in front of the Tower of Terror.
- There is a FastPass+ kiosk to the right of the Muppets attraction.
- There is a FastPass+ kiosk next to Toy Story Midway Mania.
- If you need to avoid crowds, get out of the heat, or just need a short cut, then go through the shops that are on the left as you exit the theme park.
- There is a walkway from the Hollywood Studios to the Boardwalk and the Boardwalk resorts. After you exit the park you will walk straight and then to the left.

Walkway from the Studios to the Boardwalk

- If you don't have the Fantasmic dining package, get in line more than an hour before Fantasmic begins to get a seat. It will fill up very fast.
- If there are two shows for Fantasmic, the later show will have fewer people in attendance. You still should get in line early.
- Do not sit in the first five rows at Fantasmic unless you want to get wet.
- If you are not going to see Fantasmic, visit any nearby attractions because the wait times will drop considerably.

Chapter 10

Epcot attraction descriptions and recommendations for different age groups & tips

Epcot Attractions

Spaceship Earth: You get to experience what it is like to ride inside of Epcot's iconic geodesic dome. You will experience how communication began and how it has developed over the years. You even get to see yourself in the future and experience what it might be like. Each car holds two people, unless a third person is very small. The wait times will vary during the day, but it is a continuously moving ride. FastPass+ is available, but not completely necessary. **Length of attraction:** 16 minutes 50 seconds. **Megan's rating: 3 & Merino's rating: 5.**

Inside Spaceship Earth (The Roman Empire Scene)

Ellen's Energy Adventure: Energy is all around us! Ellen's Energy Adventure is in the Universe of Energy pavilion and it is a lot of fun. You will enjoy a pre-show which stars comedian, Ellen DeGeneres, playing Jeopardy. She is having a tough time answering questions, so she gets a visit from "Bill Nye the Science Guy" to assist her. You then move into the main area where you ride in very large vehicles and go along with Ellen to learn about energy. She goes all the way back to the age of the dinosaurs. There is usually no wait since the vehicles seat a large number of people. It is a great attraction to go on when waiting for your FastPass+ time at another attraction. Be aware that the show lasts approximately 45 minutes. **Megan's rating: 4 & Merino's rating: 4.**

Mission: Space: This attraction is a definite must see in Epcot! You and your family will ride in a space shuttle and blast off to Mars. Everyone has a different role in the space shuttle, so pay attention to your responsibility. There are two different intensities of the ride. The green team is less intense on the body. You will experience a milder mission, but you will have the same adventure. The orange team is very intense because of all the G forces on the body. I have experienced the orange side of the attraction once. Mind you I have never had a problem going on any ride before, anywhere. However, when I selected the orange team and the ride began I started to feel sick. I began sweating and all I could think of was "please make this ride stop!" When I finally got off, I was not able to do anything for about two hours. The height requirement is 44" and FastPass+ is available. However, the wait in the standby line is typically around 20 to 30 minutes during the day. **Length of attraction:** 6 minutes. **Megan's rating: 4 & Merino's rating: 5.**

Inside the ship for Mission: Space

Test Track: As my son Merino would say, "That was AWESOME!" You experience what cars go through before they are sold, as you design your own custom vehicle that travels through a testing facility. Your test car goes over bumps, around turns, and up to 65 miles per hour in this open air vehicle. The height requirement is 40" and FastPass+ is available. I would recommend going to Test Track very early. The FastPass+ times go quickly, and the standby line will get up to over an hour by noon. **Length of attraction:** 4 minutes 45 seconds. **Megan's rating: 4 & Merino's rating: 5.**

Riding in the Test Track vehicle

Journey into Imagination with Figment: The attraction is located in the Imagination Pavilion of Epcot. You experience a journey with a fun loving character named Figment. The journey will take you through many "labs" and will test all of your senses. FastPass+ is available, but do not waste one on this attraction, since the wait for the attraction will be minimal. **Length of**

attraction: 6 minutes 50 seconds. **Megan's rating: 2 & Merino's rating: 2.**

Imagination Pavilion

Disney & Pixar Short Film Festival: You and your family will experience three animated shorts that are in spectacular 4D! The theater is a good size and there are even in-theater effects. FastPass+ is available. **Length of attraction:** 18 minutes.

Soarin: Soarin is another must see in Epcot that is located in the Land Pavilion. When you enter the pavilion go to the right and follow the walkway. Then, take the stairs down and turn to the right. When you do get on the attraction, you sit in a ski lift style seat. You feel the rush of the wind in your hair, experience the smell of trees, see and feel the ocean as you fly overhead. It is a sensory experience you must do. The height requirement is 40" and FastPass+ is available. This attraction is very popular, so visit it when Epcot opens if you do not have a FastPass+ time. The truth is, by mid - morning the standby wait time will be up to an hour or two wait or even longer. **Length of attraction:** 4 minutes 45 seconds. **Megan's rating 3: & Merino's rating: 3.**

Soarin

Living with the Land: Can it be fun to learn on a vacation? When it comes to "Living with the Land" it can be possible. This attraction is located in the Land Pavilion. You will ride in a boat and visit greenhouses where the vegetables are grown that are used in the Epcot restaurants. You will experience a fish farm that Disney has developed as well. FastPass+ is available, but it is not necessary. **Length of attraction:** 15 minutes. **Megan's rating: 2 & Merino's rating: 3.**

Riding on Living with the Land

The Circle of Life: You sit in a large theater to watch a film featuring the characters from the movie “The Lion King,” as you learn about the Earth and its cycles. It is an entertaining attraction to visit when you are waiting for your FastPass+ time for Soarin, since it is located in the Land Pavilion. There is usually little to no wait. **Length of attraction:** 12 minutes 40 seconds. **Megan's rating: 2 & Merino's rating: 3.**

The Seas with Nemo & Friends: Your family will travel into the world of Nemo. You ride in a clam style vehicle and travel along with Nemo's friends as they are trying to locate where he has gone. The wait can be 30 minutes during the day, and the ride is only a few minutes long. However, when you get off the ride you go into the Seas with Nemo & Friends area and experience all types of sea life. FastPass+ is available. **Length of attraction:** 5 minutes 50 seconds. **Megan's rating: 2 & Merino's rating: 2.**

Fish in the Seas with Nemo & Friends

Turtle Talk with Crush: This is a magnificent attraction inside the Seas with Nemo & Friends Pavilion. You will sit in a small theater and all the kids get to sit right in front of the screen. Crush, from the movie "Finding Nemo," will appear on the screen and interact with the kids directly. Children can ask Crush questions, and he will answer which is impressive! The wait time is typically around 30 minutes, but well worth it if you do not have a FastPass+ time. **Megan's rating: 4 & Merino's rating: 3.**

Epcot Character Spot: Here is the place to have your children meet, take pictures with, and get autographs from Mickey and all his pals! It is located in Future World next to Innoventions East and West. FastPass+ is available.

The Sum of All Thrills: You will finally have the chance to actually design your own thrill ride! You can choose to design your own roller coaster, jet plane, or bobsled experience. You can make the experience as intense as you want. If it gets too intense, you have the choice to stop the simulator during the ride. The minimum height requirement is 48" and it is located near the Electric Umbrella in Innoventions East. **Length of attraction:** 2 minutes 30 seconds. **Megan's rating 4: & Merino's rating: 4.**

Sum of All Thrills

Habit Heroes: This is a fun filled family attraction. You will become a Habit Hero and fight monsters such as Dehydration. The attraction is interactive as you move around a room and become a Hero to the planet. It is located in Innoventions East directly across from The Sum of All Thrills. There is typically little wait for Habit Heroes. **Length of attraction:** 20 minutes. **Megan's rating: 3 & Merino's rating: 4.**

Gran Fiesta Tour Starring the Three Caballeros: This is a calm boat ride through Mexico, which is located in World Showcase. You will learn about Mexican culture and see a film starring Donald Duck. The wait time will not be long. **Length of attraction:** 8 minutes 20 seconds. **Megan's rating: 2 & Merino's rating: 2.**

The Three Caballeros

Epcot shows

Disney Phineas & Ferb: Agent P's World Showcase Adventure: If your child enjoys Phineas & Ferb, then they will love this interactive experience. Your child will become a secret agent and use a high tech device to find clues throughout World Showcase. They eventually will help Agent P, Perry the Platypus, defeat Dr. Doofenshmirtz. **Megan's rating: 4 & Merino's rating: 4.**

Illuminations: This is a must see night time celebration of cultures in World Showcase! Find an area to stand anywhere around World Showcase to view a breathtaking firework display synchronized to exhilarating music. There is even a gigantic globe, with television screens embedded in it, that has a surprise ending. The show runs nightly and usually begins at 9pm. FastPass+ is available, but there are numerous locations to see the show. I also would not use one of your initial three FastPass+ selections on Illuminations because you would not be able to get a 4th FastPass+ during your visit to Epcot.

My Recommendations for Epcot attractions to see with young children ages 1-7

- Test Track (40" to ride) ***FastPass+ available - use child swap***

- Ellen's Energy Adventure
- Mission: Space (44" to ride) ***FastPass+ available - use child swap***
- Spaceship Earth ***FastPass+ available***

Spaceship Earth

- Living with the Land ***FastPass+ available***
- The Circle of Life
- Soarin (40" to ride) ***FastPass+ available - use child swap***
- Epcot Character Spot ***FastPass+ available***
- The Seas with Nemo & Friends ***FastPass+ available***
- Turtle Talk with Crush ***FastPass+ available***
- Journey Into Imagination with Figment ***FastPass+**

available*

- Disney & Pixar Short Film Festival ***FastPass+ available***
- Innoventions East and West (explore these two areas of technology and science)
- Habit Heroes
- Disney Phineas & Ferb: Agent P's World Showcase Adventure
- Gran Fiesta Tour Starring The Three Caballeros
- Reflections of China (watch a movie about China in this Circle – Vision 360 film)
- Visit Germany
- Visit Italy
- Visit American Adventure (show about the history of the United States)
- Visit Japan
- Visit Morocco
- Impressions de France (enjoy a film about France)
- Visit United Kingdom
- Canada (watch this Circle – Vision 360 film about Canada)

Epcot shows

- Illuminations: Reflections of Earth ***FastPass+ available***

My Top 5 Must See Attractions in Epcot for ages 1-7

1) The Seas with Nemo & Friends
2) Turtle Talk with Crush
3) Spaceship Earth
4) Soarin
5) Disney & Pixar Short Film Festival

My Recommendations for Epcot attractions to see with children ages 8-12

- Test Track (40" to ride) ***FastPass+ available***
- Mission: Space (44" to ride) ***FastPass+ available***

Navigator seat in Mission: Space

- Ellen's Energy Adventure
- Spaceship Earth ***FastPass+ available***
- Living with the Land ***FastPass+ available***
- The Circle of Life
- Soarin (40" to ride) ***FastPass+ available***
- Epcot Character Spot ***FastPass+ available***
- The Seas with Nemo & Friends ***FastPass+ available***
- Turtle Talk with Crush ***FastPass+ available***
- Journey Into Imagination with Figment ***FastPass+ available***
- Disney & Pixar Short Film Festival ***FastPass+ available***
- Innoventions East and West (explore these two areas of technology and science)
- The Sum of All Thrills (48" to ride)
- Habit Heroes

Habit Heroes

- Disney Phineas & Ferb: Agent P's World Showcase Adventure
- Gran Fiesta Tour Starring The Three Caballeros
- Reflections of China (watch a movie about China in this Circle - Vision 360 film)
- Visit Germany
- Visit Italy
- Visit American Adventure (show about the history of the United States)
- Visit Japan
- Visit Morocco
- Impressions de France (enjoy a film about France)
- Visit United Kingdom
- Canada (watch this Circle – Vision 360 film about Canada)

Epcot shows

- Illuminations: Reflections of Earth ***FastPass+ available***

My Top 5 Must See Attractions in Epcot for ages 8-12

1) Test Track
2) Mission: Space
3) Soarin
4) Ellen's Energy Adventure
5) The Sum of All Thrills

My Recommendations for Epcot attractions to see with children ages 13-17 & adults only

Fountain in Epcot

- Test Track (40“ to ride) ***FastPass+ available***
- Mission: Space (44” to ride) ***FastPass+ available***

Mission: Space

- Ellen's Energy Adventure
- Spaceship Earth ***FastPass+ available***
- Living with the Land ***FastPass+ available***
- The Circle of Life
- Soarin (40" to ride) ***FastPass+ available***
- The Sum of All Thrills (48" to ride)
- Habit Heroes
- The Seas with Nemo & Friends Pavilion
- Disney & Pixar Short Film Festival ***FastPass+ available***
- Innoventions East and West (explore these two areas of technology and science)
- Epcot Character Spot ***FastPass+ available***
- Gran Fiesta Tour Starring The Three Caballeros
- Reflections of China (watch a movie about China in this Circle - Vision 360 film)
- Visit Germany
- Visit Italy
- Visit American Adventure (show about the history of the United States)
- Visit Japan
- Visit Morocco
- Impressions de France (enjoy a film about France)
- Visit United Kingdom

- Canada (watch this Circle – Vision 360 film about Canada)

Epcot shows

- Illuminations: Reflections of Earth ***FastPass+ available***

My Top 5 Must See Attractions in Epcot for ages 13-17 & adults only

1) Test Track
2) Mission: Space
3) Soarin
4) Ellen's Energy Adventure
5) The Sum of All Thrills

Epcot Tips

- Epcot's regular park hours are from 9am to 9pm.
- Arrive 30 minutes before Epcot opens to ride Soarin or Test Track, whichever one you did not make as a FastPass+ selection.
- FastPass+ times can possibly be gone for Soarin and Test Track by 11am or earlier for the entire day. The wait in the regular line for these attractions could be well over an hour without FastPass+.
- If you have an early FastPass+ time at Soarin, there is a food court next to Soarin called Sunshine Seasons where

you can get breakfast.

- While waiting for your Soarin FastPass+ time, you could visit Living with the Land and the Circle of Life.

The Land Pavilion (contains Soarin)

- Epcot is a very large theme park, and you will probably do the most walking in this park. Make sure you have comfortable sneakers or shoes.
- There is a Starbucks in the Fountain View Café.

Fountain View

- Mission: Space and Test Track are next to each other. You can use a FastPass+ for Test Track first and then go on Mission: Space.
- Test Track does have a single rider line that is shorter than the regular line if you do not have a FastPass+. However, even if your party all goes in the single rider line, you will not ride together.
- During the pre-show of Test Track you will design a car that is saved to your MagicBand. Make sure you scan your MagicBand again before you ride Test Track to see how your vehicle performs.
- After you exit your Test Track vehicle you will see an area called Photo Finish! You can have three pictures taken with various backgrounds and the pictures can be sent to an email address. You can design a commercial too!
- Mission: Space has two ways to experience the attraction.

The orange training side is very intense and may get you sick. I recommend going on the green training side that is not as intense. You get to see the same attraction going on either one, but the green has less G forces on your body.

Green Team Ticket for Mission: Space

- At the end of Mission: Space you will enter a room where you can email a video message of your family to anyone you choose.
- At the end of Mission: Space you can play astronaut video games and your children can climb through tubes.
- Visit the Art of Disney store. They sell Disney art and there are times when a Disney animator is on hand.

The Art of Disney

- If you have little ones, bring a bathing suit and towel with you. There are a few areas that have splash fountains. These are areas where water comes right up out of the ground. There is one near Test Track.
- You can either enter The Seas with Nemo & Friends by going on the Nemo ride or going through the Nemo exit, which is on the left.
- Explore The Seas with Nemo & Friends and check out all of the aquarium areas.
- Spaceship Earth has a great view of the stars and a fascinating way at the end of the ride to send a picture of your party to an email address.
- There is a walkway to the Boardwalk area from World Showcase. It is only a 5 minute walk to get to the Boardwalk area resorts.

Sign for the walkway to the Epcot Resorts

- There is an entrance at the back of Epcot from the Boardwalk resorts.
- If you need to get off your feet while watching the pre-show for Ellen's Energy Adventure, there are a few benches against the back wall.
- While waiting to enter the Circle of Life attraction you can sit on benches that are against the back wall to take a load off.
- Check out Club Cool! You can taste soda from all over the world for free!

Club Cool

- There is a FastPass+ kiosk between the Electric Umbrella and MouseGear.
- There is a FastPass+ kiosk between the Character Spot and the walkway to the Land.
- There is a FastPass+ kiosk in the International Gateway in front of the World Traveler shop.
- Grab lunch, dessert, or a snack in a country in World Showcase.
- The adults in the family should try the grand marnier and grey goose orange slush at Les Vins des Chefs de France in the France Pavilion. It is a frozen wine drink.
- The adults in the family could try numerous types of alcoholic drinks in World Showcase.
- The Circle Vision 360 theaters in certain countries do not have seats because the film is all around you.
- In Japan you can purchase a Pokémon stuffed animal for

your child in the gift shop.

- If needed, there are restrooms on your left after you have exited Epcot and are walking towards the resort buses.
- Book a dining reservation at the Rose and Crown around 8pm. When you check in ask to be seated near the windows to have an up close viewing of Illuminations.
- Make sure you see the incredible night time show called Illuminations: Reflections of Earth. You can view it anywhere in World Showcase. Try to pick a place near Canada so you are not too far from the exit.

Illuminations

Chapter 11

The Wait Time is Too Long!

"Mom, I am not waiting for an hour!" I have seen, heard, and experienced this too many times in Walt Disney World. Families walk up to an attraction and the standby wait time is well over a reasonable time. So, what do you do now?

This is exactly why I decided to write this chapter. This section of my book will assist you when wait times are ridiculous at an attraction and the kids are about to completely melt down. I am also assuming the FastPass+ times for the given attraction are gone for the day. If they are available, then obtain a FastPass+ time. You obviously could always wait in the standby line too.

I will begin in the **Magic Kingdom.** What if you walk over to **Space Mountain** and the wait time is horrible? You could:

- Ride the Tomorrowland Transit Authority PeopleMover.
- See the Carousel of Progress.
- See Stitch's Great Escape!
- Ride Buzz Lightyear.
- Eat lunch or dinner at the Starlight Cafe.
- Ride the Mad Tea Party in Fantasyland.

What if you walk into Fantasyland and the wait time for **Peter Pan** is so long that your kids want to cry? You could:

- Enter It's a Small World if the wait time is 20 minutes or less.

- See Mickey's PhilharMagic.
- Go over and experience the Haunted Mansion.
- Ride the Carrousel.
- Eat lunch or dinner at Pinocchio Village Haus.

Let's say you remain in Fantasyland and your children want to ride **The Many Adventures of Winnie the Pooh.** When you get to the attraction the wait is the same time you experience while waiting to finally hear your name called at the doctor's office. You could:

- Ride the Mad Tea Party.
- Experience Mickey's PhilharMagic.
- Grab an ice cream at Storybook Treats.
- Ride the Carrousel.
- Get something to eat at Pinocchio's Village Haus or Be Our Guest Restaurant.

Your family decides to experience the timeless classic, **Dumbo.** However, when you arrive at Dumbo the wait time is at the "OMG" level. You could:

- Go in Pete's Silly Sideshow to have your picture taken with the characters.
- Experience Mickey's PhilharMagic.
- Take the kids in the Casey Jr. Splash 'N' Soak Station.
- Ride the Walt Disney World Railroad.
- Grab a treat at Gaston's Tavern.

You are still in Fantasyland and you go to **The Barnstormer featuring Goofy as the Great Goffini.** Let's say, for the sake of argument that the wait time is approximately 45 minutes. You could:

- Ride Dumbo if the line is short.
- Have the kids play in Casey Jr. Splash 'N' Soak Station.
- Visit Pete's Silly Sideshow and have your picture taken with the characters.
- Experience Mickey's PhilharMagic.
- Ride the Mad Tea Party.

Your family now wants to visit the New Fantasyland and ride **Under the Sea: Journey of the Little Mermaid.** You notice that the wait time is the same as one of your children's tee ball games. Instead of waiting you could:

- Experience Enchanted Tales with Belle if the wait time is minimal.
- Have your picture taken with Ariel in Ariel's Grotto.
- Visit the shops in Belle's village.
- Go into Gaston's Tavern, take a load off, have snack, and get LeFou's Brew.
- Take the kids to play in Casey Jr. Splash 'N' Soak Station.
- See Mickey's PhilharMagic.

The family is now yelling that they want to ride the **Seven Dwarfs Mine Train.** You get to the standby line and it mirrors the amount of time it took to cook a holiday turkey. So you could:

- See Mickey's PhilharMagic.
- Ride It's a Small World if the wait time is minimal.
- Experience Peter Pan's Flight if the wait time is reasonable.
- Go over to the Mad Tea Party.
- Eat lunch at the Be Our Guest restaurant.
- Eat lunch or dinner at Pinocchio's Village Haus.

You decide it is time to see Belle and experience **Enchanted Tales with Belle.** You notice that the wait time is similar to the time it will take to fly to France and actually see Belle's home country. So, you could:

- Ride Under the Sea: Journey of the Little Mermaid if the wait time is minimal.
- Grab a snack at Gaston's Tavern.
- Have your picture taken with Ariel.
- Experience Mickey's PhilharMagic.
- Go over to Storybook Circus and explore the area.

The children now want to have their picture taken with and meet Anna, Elsa, or Cinderella. However, when you get over to Princess Fairytale Hall the wait time is actually 180 minutes long! Yes, I sadly have actually seen this long of a wait time. The family does have options. They are:

- Ride the Carrousel.
- See Mickey's PhilharMagic.

- Experience Peter Pan's Flight or It's a Small World if wait times are minimal.
- Ride Winnie the Pooh.
- Wander over to Tomorrowland and see the Monster's Inc. Laugh Floor.

Your family is now in Frontierland and they want to ride **Splash Mountain.** You look up at the wait time and wonder if it will still be daylight when you finally get to the front of the line. So, instead of waiting you could:

- Go on Big Thunder Mountain Railroad if the wait is 20 minutes or less.
- Ride the Jungle Cruise.
- Experience Pirates of the Caribbean.
- Ride the Walt Disney World Railroad.
- Eat lunch or dinner at Pecos Bill Tall Tale Inn and Cafe.
- Walk over to the Haunted Mansion and go on.

Your family has now walked next door to the attraction **Big Thunder Mountain Railroad.** You notice that the standby wait time is comparable to the length of your favorite movie. So, you do have options. You could:

- Ride Splash Mountain if the wait is 20 minutes or less.
- Ride the Jungle Cruise if the wait is 20 minutes or less.
- Experience Pirates of the Caribbean.
- Ride the Walt Disney World Railroad.
- Eat lunch or dinner at Pecos Bill Tall Tale Inn and Cafe.

- Go in the Hall of Presidents.
- Walk over to the Haunted Mansion and visit the ghosts.

You make your way into Adventureland and want to ride the **Jungle Cruise.** The wait time happens to be the same time it would take to actually build your own cruise boat. So, you could:

- Ride the Pirates of the Caribbean.
- Ride The Magic Carpets of Aladdin.
- Try to go on Splash Mountain or Big Thunder Mountain if the wait times are short.
- Eat lunch or dinner at Pecos Bill Tall Tale Inn and Cafe.

Now we will travel over to **Disney's Hollywood Studios.** The whole family wants to go on **The Twilight Zone Tower of Terror.** You decide it is a great idea, but it is late in the day. You finally get over to the Hollywood Hotel and notice that the wait time is the same number as the age of your great grandmother. You decide it is much too long. So you could:

- See a Beauty and the Beast show if the next show is starting within 30 minutes.
- Check the wait time at Rock 'n' Roller Coaster and go on if the wait is 20 minutes or less.
- Grab a coffee or a pastry at the small stand outside of the Tower of Terror gift shop exit.
- Experience the Great Movie Ride.
- See the Voyage of the Little Mermaid.
- Eat lunch or dinner at Rosie's All-American Cafe.

The **Rock 'n' Roller Coaster Starring Aerosmith** is now a top priority that your family wants to experience. You wander over to the standby line and look up to see the wait time. The number is higher than the speed limit on I-4. So, instead of waiting in line you could:

- Ride the Tower of Terror if the wait is 20 minutes or less.
- See a Beauty and the Beast show if a show time is coming up soon.
- Go on the Great Movie Ride.
- See Ariel sing at the Voyage of the Little Mermaid.
- Eat lunch or dinner at Rosie's All-American Cafe.

One of the most popular attractions in the Hollywood Studios is **Toy Story Midway Mania.** The wait time is always considerable. It can be as long as 120 minutes or even more. If you decide not to wait you could:

- Experience the Voyage of the Little Mermaid.
- Ride the Great Movie Ride.
- Visit Walt Disney: One Man's Dream.
- Eat lunch or dinner at Sci – Fi Dine in Theater Restaurant.

Toy Story Midway Mania wait time

Another attraction in the Studios where you may encounter a long wait is **Star Tours.** So, what could you do if the wait time is at a ridiculous level? Well, you could:

- Experience Muppet Vision 3D.
- See a Jedi Training Academy show.
- Take in an Indiana Jones show if a show time is coming up soon.

Indiana Jones

- Experience the Great Movie Ride.
- Shop in the Star Tours shop, which is to the right of the entrance.
- Eat lunch or dinner at the Backlot Express.

We will next travel over to **EPCOT.** What if the wait time at **Soarin** is in the triple digits? You could:

- Ride the attraction named Living with the Land.
- See the attraction The Circle of Life.
- Walk over to The Seas with Nemo and Friends.
- Eat a meal at Sunshine Seasons.

Your family now wants to experience **Mission: Space.**

You look at the wait time and realize that your stomach is growling. You decide that if you wait in the line you may not eat for an hour. So you could:

- Experience Test Track if the wait time is reasonable.
- Visit the exhibits at Innoventions East.
- Walk over to the Universe of Energy and see Ellen's Energy Adventure.
- Eat lunch or dinner at the Electric Umbrella.

A very popular attraction in EPCOT that may have long wait times is **Test Track.** So what else could you do if the standby line is at the “Wow” level? You could:

- Ride Mission: Space if the wait is 20 minutes or less.
- Walk over and experience Ellen's Energy Adventure.
- Visit the exhibits at Innoventions East.
- Eat lunch or dinner at the Electric Umbrella.

We will finally travel over to **Disney's Animal Kingdom.** You enter the Africa section and want to experience **Kilimanjaro Safaris.** What if the wait time is comparable to a nine hole round of golf? You could:

- Explore the Pangani Forest Exploration Trail.
- Grab something to eat at the Tusker House Restaurant.
- Walk over to Asia and ride Kali River Rapids if the wait is 20 minutes or less.
- Take in a Festival of the Lion King show if a show is beginning soon.

Your family now wants to see the Yeti and ride **Expedition Everest** in Asia. You get over to the attraction and notice that people are everywhere. The wait time is how long it would take to count all the pennies in your house. So, you could:

- Explore Maharajah Jungle Trek.
- See a Flights of Wonder show if a show is upcoming.
- Ride Kali River Rapids.
- Walk over to Dinoland U.S.A. and ride Dinosaur or explore the area.
- Eat lunch or dinner at the Yak & Yeti Restaurant.

Riding Expedition Everest

You remain in Asia and really want to get wet so everyone decides to ride **Kali River Rapids.** In my experience, the wait times here are typically not as long as some of the other attractions. But for the sake of argument, what if the wait time is as long as the nap you want to take soon? You could:

- Ride Expedition Everest if the wait time is 20 minutes or less.
- Explore Maharajah Jungle Trek.
- Check the show times and see a Flights of Wonder show.
- Walk over to Africa and ride Kilimanjaro Safaris if the wait time is reasonable.

You now want to see a T-Rex or any dinosaur so you enter Dinoland U.S.A. **Dinosaur** is a very popular attraction and you realize quickly that this day is no different. The wait time feels like the length of time it has been since dinosaurs roamed the Earth. Instead of waiting you could:

- Ride Primeval Whirl.
- Take the kids to play over at The Boneyard.
- Ride TriceraTop Spin.
- Play the carnival style games in Dinoland.

Dino-Rama games

- Eat lunch or dinner at Restaurantosaurus.

Your family wants to spin and spin on **Primeval Whirl.** You get to the attraction and you might as well pull up a cozy chair. The wait time is just as long as your parent's lecture when you were getting a driver's license. You decide it is just too long, so you could:

- Experience Dinosaur if the wait time is 20 minutes or less.
- Take the kids over to play at The Boneyard.
- Play carnival style games in Dinoland.
- Ride TriceraTop Spin.
- Eat lunch or dinner at Restaurantosaurus.

Walt Disney World is a truly magical place. Please do not assume now that wait times will always be awful and FastPass+ times will be gone in minutes. The chapter is only hypothetical, and it will help when you happen to be in a theme park during an incredibly busy day, or if you have arrived at a theme park very late in the day. The kids and big kids at heart will be happy you have read this chapter.

Chapter 12

Walt Disney World Tips

(Transportation, money saving, resort, general, baby/young child, and relaxing days)

Transportation Tips

- You do not need to rent a car if you are staying in a Walt Disney World Resort. Disney will take you everywhere within their property lines.
- There is no additional cost to use Disney Transportation.

Magic Kingdom bus

- Use Disney's Magical Express service, and let Disney get your bags for you if you are traveling into and from

Orlando International Airport.

- After you land in Orlando International Airport it typically takes an hour and a half to arrive in your resort if you are using Disney's Magical Express.
- If you use Magical Express, be aware that Disney will pick you up to return to Orlando International Airport three hours before your flight departs.
- When you are waiting for Disney's Magical Express to return you to the airport, be aware that the bus could say: Disney's Magical Express, Disney Cruise Line, or Mears. Make sure you ask the driver so you do not miss your shuttle to return home.
- When you are going to a theme park, go to the bus stop areas in your resort. The buses will have the name of the theme park they are traveling to on the front.
- Disney buses run every 15 to 20 minutes.
- When you are leaving a theme park to return to your resort, go to the bus stop area and find the correct stop for your resort.
- If you are traveling from one resort to another, you need to take a bus to Disney Springs or a theme park, and then take a bus to the resort destination from there. Allow around 1 hour for travel time.
- If you have an early dining reservation in a theme park before the park opens, you can still use Disney

transportation. Disney buses begin to operate at approximately 6:45am for certain theme parks. Ask the front desk for when the first bus will arrive.

- If you have an early dining reservation at a resort, you can still use Disney Transportation. The buses do operate early. Take a bus to a theme park or Disney Springs, and go to the resort from there. Check with your resort front desk for the first time a bus will arrive. Also, ask the bus driver if you can be dropped off at your resort destination. If they are able, the driver will bring you to the resort.
- You can travel from theme park to theme park by using either the Disney buses, boats, or the monorail. The monorail goes between the Magic Kingdom and Epcot.
- If you are at the Magic Kingdom and want to get to Epcot, take the monorail labelled Epcot.
- If you are at the Magic Kingdom and want to travel to Disney's Animal Kingdom or Disney's Hollywood Studios, take the monorail to the Transportation and Ticket Center (TTC). You will take the correct bus from there.
- When traveling from the Hollywood Studios to the Magic Kingdom, take a bus to the Transportation and Ticket Center (TTC). Then, get on the monorail to the Magic Kingdom.
- When traveling from the Hollywood Studios to Epcot, take a bus directly to Epcot or to the TTC. Then, get on

the monorail to Epcot from there. You can also take a boat. The boat will take you to the Swan, Dolphin, Yacht Club, Beach Club, and Boardwalk as well.

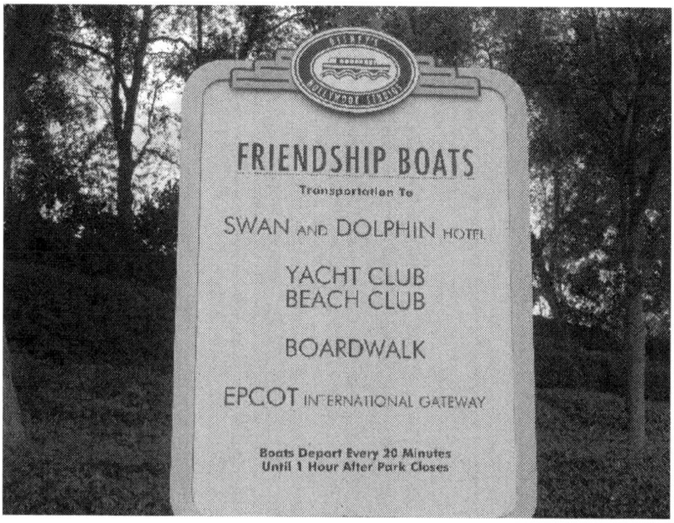

Transportation sign from Studios to Epcot

- When traveling from the Hollywood Studios to Disney's Animal Kingdom, take a bus directly to Animal Kingdom or to the TTC. Take the Animal Kingdom bus from there.
- If you are leaving Disney's Animal Kingdom and want to travel to the Magic Kingdom, Epcot, or Disney's Hollywood Studios, go to the bus stops and find the correct bus stop to take you to your destination.
- If you want to go from Epcot to the Magic Kingdom, take the express monorail to the Magic Kingdom. You will then take another monorail to the Magic Kingdom.

Monorail

- If you want to travel from Epcot to Disney's Animal Kingdom or Disney's Hollywood Studios, take the monorail to the TTC. You will then take a bus to either theme park from there.
- If you drive to the theme parks, it costs $20 to park if you are not a Walt Disney World Resort guest. If you are a Disney resort guest, it is free.
- To get to the Hoop Dee Doo Musical Revue at Disney's Fort Wilderness take a boat from the Magic Kingdom. Look for the sign at the boat launch area.
- You can get back and forth to the Grand Floridian and the Polynesian from the Magic Kingdom by taking a boat. When you exit the Magic Kingdom walk towards the

water and go to the right. Look for the sign that says "Resort Launches."

- The Transportation and Ticket Center (TTC) is a stop on the monorail loop. You can get to all of the theme parks from the TTC by using Walt Disney World transportation.
- The Contemporary Resort, Polynesian Resort, and the Grand Floridian are all on the monorail loop that connects to the Magic Kingdom. The order of stops on the monorail after you leave the Magic Kingdom are: The Contemporary, Transportation and Ticket Center (TTC), Polynesian, and Grand Floridian.
- Whenever you eat dinner at a resort that is not your own, and you do not want to take two buses to get back to your resort, then go to the valet desk in front of the resort. Ask the cast member to call a taxi. It will cost around $10 to $20, but it is at least an hour time saver.
- You can rent a car on WDW property by calling the Car Care Center at (407) 824-3470. Alamo and National are in the Car Care Center and it is located near the Magic Kingdom. The Car Care Center offers complimentary shuttle service to and from WDW resort hotels.

Money Saving Tips

- Stay in a value resort as opposed to a moderate resort. You will save hundreds of dollars and still have a terrific time.

- Stay in a moderate resort as opposed to a deluxe resort. For a seven night stay you could save thousands of dollars.
- When it comes to the Magic Your Way Tickets, do not purchase the water park and more option. This will be a savings of $64 per ticket.
- If your vacation is planned out where you do not have to park hop, then do not add on the park hopper option to your Magic Your Way Ticket. This will be a savings of $64 per ticket.
- Purchase the dining plan I recommended. You will save around 20% on dining in Walt Disney World. You will also receive a refillable mug with the plan. This will be a huge savings when it comes to beverages.
- Save about $154 for the week on water. Here is the way to do it. Go to any counter service area and ask them for tap water and ice in a cup when you are thirsty. They will give it to you for no charge. The $154 savings amount was determined using this scenario. Bottled water is $2.75 per bottle. Let's say you have a family of four and everyone drinks two bottles of water a day, which adds up to $22 per day. $22 per day for 7 days is $154.
- If it is possible, travel to Walt Disney World during an off peak time such as September or January, with the

exception of Martin Luther King, Jr. weekend. You can save hundreds or even thousands of dollars depending where you stay. Since I am now an Authorized Disney Vacation Planner and travel agent you can contact me directly to discuss this idea and I can book your entire trip for you. My email is jmerola@mousevacationplanning.com. My website is www.mousevacationplanning.com.

- Be on the lookout for free dining. Walt Disney World Resort offers this sporadically throughout the year. It will save you hundreds of dollars. So you know, free dining is usually not offered during a busy time of year.
- Sign up for the Disney Visa card. You will earn $1 for every $100 spent. The dollars you earn can be transferred to a Disney redemptions rewards card and used anywhere within WDW. Visit www.disneyrewards.com.
- If you are in the military you can obtain a military room only discount. The offer is typically about 25% off rooms at value resorts, 30% off at moderate resorts, and 40% off at deluxe resorts. The discount is for select rooms only and you will need to show your military ID at check in.

Resort Tips

- When you check into your resort, a cast member will ask you if you would like charging privileges connected to your MagicBand. This is a great option to have because you can use your MagicBand as a credit card anywhere in Walt Disney World. You will not have to carry cash or a credit card.

- Make sure the cast member checking you in has you create a 4 digit pin number that is connected to your MagicBand. This is very important for security. If your MagicBand gets misplaced or lost, no one can charge anything to your room without knowing the 4 digit pin number.
- If you have more than one MagicBand from previous vacations, make sure you have the cast member checking you in scan your current MagicBand. You want to be sure the MagicBand will open your resort room door. Please insist on it.
- Your MagicBand will act as the following: your Disney's Magical Express reservation, your resort room key, your ticket to enter the theme parks, a credit card if you have charging privileges, FastPass+ ticket, and your dining plan card if you choose a Disney dining plan.
- Kids can watch classic Disney cartoons while you check in at any resort. Look for couches and chairs near a TV.
- While waiting for your table at Cape May in the Beach Club, your kids can watch Disney cartoons in the lobby.
- When you arrive in your resort room take a picture of your

room number with your phone so you remember when returning from your first day in the theme parks.

- Make sure to use the in-room safe to lock up valuables.
- Set a Wake Up call from your resort room phone. A Disney character will call the room to get everyone up.
- There are very clean public restrooms in all of Walt Disney World. Three of the best are at the Beach Club outside of Cape May, inside the ESPN Club which contains televisions too, and in the Contemporary Resort at Chef Mickey's.
- All WDW resorts show a night time Disney movie for everyone. Be sure to ask when and where the movie will be shown.
- There is a resort on Walt Disney World property called the Shades of Green Resort. It is for United States Military members and their families to vacation in Walt Disney World. It is owned by the Department of Defense. The rates for a standard room are $98 - $138. You can make reservations by calling (888) 593-2242. Their website is www.shadesofgreen.org.
- There are military discounts on theme park tickets. The deal right now is a 4 day park hopper ticket for $196. Check www.shadesofgreen.org for any other discounts.
- There is a walkway between Disney's Art of Animation Resort and Disney's Pop Century Resort. It is in the back

of both resorts.

- If you visit Disney's Port Orleans Riverside Resort go to the River Roost Lounge to be entertained by the piano player Bob Jackson. He plays there four or five nights a week.
- If you need a dining reservation or need to modify one, then go to the concierge desk at your Walt Disney World resort and ask for help. They will have better luck making a dining reservation. Try this at about 9pm for the next day because some reservations may open due to the fact that guests have to cancel dining reservations the night before a reservation.
- At Fort Wilderness, the kids can play on the playground while waiting for your dining time at Mickey's BBQ or the Hoop Dee Doo Musical Revue.
- While at Fort Wilderness you can take a boat to the Magic Kingdom. There is a different boat that will take you to the Wilderness Lodge or the Contemporary Resort.
- If you are switching resorts you can transfer your luggage. All you have to do is visit bell services and they will take care of it.

General Tips

- Before you depart for WDW, check disneyworld.com to see what theme parks have the extra magic hour in the morning. Make sure to only visit that theme park if you are arriving early.

- Take pictures of your FastPass+ selections and your dining reservations that are on your mydisneyexperience account. This is just in case the mydisneyexperience app gives you problems in the theme parks.
- Pack your MagicBands in your carry-on bag if you are flying to WDW.
- When you get off the plane put your MagicBands on. They will be needed to check in for Disney's Magical Express.
- Try your best to arrive at a theme park when it opens. You want to get going early in Walt Disney World to get ahead of the crowds.
- Before you eat dinner in a theme park, obtain a FastPass+ for an attraction that is in the vicinity.
- The mydisneyexperience app is a big help when you need to change FastPass+ times or attractions for the next day. My daughter was exhausted one night and we had a FastPass+ time for 9:10 – 10:10 the next morning. I quickly went on the app and made the change to later in the morning.
- When you are waiting to order at a counter service restaurant, always look for the shortest line which will be on the far right or left. This also applies when you are

entering a theme park.

- If you are visiting during a family member's birthday, make sure to visit any theme park guest relations or Walt Disney World resort front desk to get a birthday pin.
- If you are visiting during the "winter months," remember to pack some sweaters, jeans, or pants. It can get cold at night.
- Look into buying an autograph book at either a resort or when you enter your first theme park. Characters will be available to sign autographs and get pictures. You want to be ready.
- Remember to pack comfortable sneakers. You will walk until your feet are yelling "no more!" in Walt Disney World.
- If you or any member of your family requires a wheelchair or Electric Convenience Vehicle (ECV), then Disney has you covered. You can rent a wheelchair for $12 per day or a length of stay rental is $10 per day. An ECV is $50 per day at any theme park.
- You can rent an ECV or wheelchair from an outside vendor. The company Disney recommends is Buena Vista Scooters. There website is buenavistascooters.com. Their phone number is 1-866-484-4797. The advantage of rental from this company is you can have your ECV or wheelchair with you at all times.

- Bring a backpack with you. It is a convenient way to carry things to the pool or the parks, such as sunscreen or snacks.
- Get a guide map and times guide when you walk into any theme park.
- After a Disney photographer takes a picture of your family they will scan your MagicBand or theme park ticket. You can view and buy the photos while on your vacation or online when you return home through your mydisneyexperience account.
- After you get off a ride that has taken your photo scan your MagicBand or theme park ticket under the photo to have it saved to your mydisneyexperience account.
- You can purchase all the photos that will be taken in Walt Disney World before your trip. It is called Memory Maker and it cost $149 before your trip or $169 after you have arrived in Disney World. This was previously named Photopass+.
- There are character meet areas in all the theme parks. Check your times guide and theme park map for information.
- Purchase Mickey ears for everyone and have their names put on the ears. Do this early, so you can pick them up before you leave the theme park. You can also purchase Mickey ears at Disney Springs.

- If you get very hot, take a break and go into any building that is near you at the time. They are all wonderfully air conditioned.
- If you have a question, do not hesitate to ask a cast member (Disney worker). They are a great help.
- Always recheck theme park hours for any possible changes at disneyworld.com or on your mydisneyexperience app.
- Walt Disney World has many different special events going on throughout the year. One of the events is called Mickey's Very Merry Christmas Party. It is a special ticket event that goes on in the Magic Kingdom on select nights in November and December. Another event in the Magic Kingdom is called Mickey's Not So Scary Halloween Party. It is also a special ticket event that happens on select nights in October.
- If you like the sound of 5K, half marathon, or marathon, then Walt Disney World has what you want. Walt Disney World offers all types of different running events. Visit rundisney.com for a schedule.
- Epcot hosts its annual International Food and Wine Festival. You can eat and drink in countries all over World Showcase and listen to great music. It typically runs from late September until mid-November. Call (407) WDW-FEST for reservations.

- The following is a list of what you should pack for your vacation: clothes for everyday and an extra set, sunglasses, sunscreen, swimsuit, cell phone and charger, camera, video camera with charger, blank dvds, all the information from Disney travel or from your travel agent, dining reservations, toiletries, children's special stuffed animals, Disney's Magical Express booklet, MagicBands, and try to get a small plastic sleeve to hold any money, etc.
- Try to visit Disney Springs the day you are departing from Walt Disney World. It will give your children one final Disney experience before they leave.
- My wife has always brought along a travel size hand sanitizer to use before meals. It is useful to have since the kids have been in many public areas.
- You can board your pet in Walt Disney World. It is called Best Friends Pet Care. It is located across from Disney's Port Orleans French Quarter. To make a reservation visit wdw.bestfriendspetcare.com or call (877) 4-WDW-PETS.
- If you are not staying in a Walt Disney World resort, do not put your theme park ticket in the same pocket as a cell phone. It will erase the metallic strip.
- If you are staying off property and do not have a MagicBand from a previous trip, you can buy one at a theme park or Disney Springs. The cast member will link the MagicBand to your mydisneyexperience account.

MagicBands for sale

- If someone gets sick while in a theme park go to the First Aid Center. You can get ibuprofen pills or liquid for the kids, and basic care. It is free.
- There are religious services near Walt Disney World. Mary, Queen of the Universe Catholic Shrine is a Catholic church, and their phone number is 407-239-6600 to call for worship service times. Community Presbyterian Church in Celebration's phone number is 407-566-1633. A Jewish celebration can be found at Celebration Jewish Congregation. Their phone number is 407-596-5397. There is the Islamic Center of Orlando, and their phone number is 407-238-2700. If you are a Mormon there is the Church of Jesus Christ of Latter Day Saints. Their

phone number is 407-909-0051. If you need a taxi to get to the service, then go to your resort bell hop and ask them to call a cab.

Baby / Young Child Tips

- **Child Swap or rider switch** is a very valuable feature Disney offers for parties who have a child who is not tall enough to go on a certain attraction. Go to the entrance of the attraction with your child and ask for a **child swap pass**. Then everyone goes on the ride except for the person who is staying with the child. The riders go through the FastPass+ entrance, if they have a FastPass+ time, or the standby entrance. When they return, the person who was waiting switches with the people who went on the ride. The person that did not go on the ride takes the **child swap pass** and can take up to three other people with them, and they go through the FastPass+ entrance. The service is free.
- You can either bring a stroller or leave it home. You can rent a stroller in all of the theme parks. A single passenger stroller cost $15 per day or $13 per day for length of stay and a double passenger stroller cost $31 per day or $27 per day for length of stay.
- My wife and I always brought along our stroller. It was more convenient while in the airport, resort, and it was a

money saver.

- All the theme parks have Baby Care Centers. They are places you can change your baby, use a microwave, clean out a bottle, watch a video, and just take a break.
- The Baby Care Centers have rocking chairs and a private place for mothers to breast feed.
- The Baby Care Centers are located in the following areas of each theme park: Magic Kingdom's Baby Care Center is to the left of Crystal Palace. In Disney's Hollywood Studios it is when you first walk in and over to the left. In Disney's Animal Kingdom it is located to the right of the Tree of Life. In Epcot it is located to the right of Test Track. I believe the Magic Kingdom has the best one. It was just right for my wife when our children were little.
- If you want to put your child down for a nap, the Disney buses run every 15 to 20 minutes to take you back to your resort.
- Many of the Walt Disney World attractions are indoors, so you will be able to get your child out of the heat or rain. The attractions have superb pre-shows to keep everyone entertained as you wait for the ride or show to start.

Tips for Relaxing days without going into a theme park

- Visit the Disney Springs area by taking a Disney bus or your car and do some shopping. Disney Springs is free and has the largest area of Disney items you will ever find. The area is an attraction in itself.
- Disney Springs has a Lego store called Lego Imagination Center.
- Disney Springs has some restaurants that do take walk-ins, depending on availability, like Planet Hollywood, Rainforest Café, and T-Rex.
- Grab a hot sandwich at Earl of Sandwich.
- Disney Springs has a delicious ice cream shop called Ghirardelli Ice Cream & Chocolate Shop.
- Visit Disney's Boardwalk area. It is free to visit. Take a bus from your resort and take it to Disney Springs. Then, get on a bus for the Boardwalk Resort or Beach Club Resort. Go into the lobby of the resort, walk through the lobby, and go out the back doors. That will take you onto the Boardwalk. The Boardwalk has street performers, places to get ice cream, a piano bar, the ESPN Club to watch a game or play games, and so much more.

Boardwalk this way!

- Go to the Beach Club Resort from the Boardwalk and get some ice cream at Beaches and Cream Soda Shop. They have incredible sundaes. They are known for one specifically named the "kitchen sink."
- Take a relaxing swim in your resort pool.
- Splitsville Bowling Alley is located at Disney Spring's West Side. Your family can bowl, listen to music, and even have a full meal served to you while you bowl.
- Disney's Grand Floridian Resort and Disney's Saratoga Springs have spas. You can book a manicure, pedicure,

massage, or facial. It also makes a great gift for mom. You can make a reservation at either spa by calling the number (407) WDW-SPAS.

Chapter 13

Location of your Favorite Character

All of your favorite characters live in Walt Disney World. No, I don't mean your favorite uncle. I mean the characters that Disney has had come to life over the years. Everyone always wants to see Mickey Mouse, Pooh Bear, Cinderella, Woody, or whoever it may be. I can still hear my kids yelling for the first time, "Mom and Dad, LOOK! There's Mickey!" This chapter will list where you can find all your favorite characters throughout Walt Disney World. **Please note:** Characters are always subject to change without notice and the times they are available is intermittent.

Mickey Mouse

- Town Square Theater in the Magic Kingdom
- Town Square area in the Magic Kingdom in the morning
- Epcot Character Spot
- Garden Grill in Epcot (restaurant)
- Near Walt Disney's: One Man Dream in the Hollywood Studios
- Near center stage in front of Great Movie Ride in the Hollywood Studios
- Adventurers Outpost in the Animal Kingdom
- Tusker House in the Animal Kingdom (restaurant)
- Chef Mickey's in the Contemporary Resort (restaurant)

- 'Ohana in the Polynesian Resort (restaurant)
- Hollywood & Vine in the Hollywood Studios (restaurant)

Minnie Mouse

- Town Square area in the Magic Kingdom in the morning
- Pete's Silly Sideshow in the Magic Kingdom
- Epcot Character Spot
- Near center stage in front of the Great Movie Ride in the Hollywood Studios
- Adventurers Outpost in the Animal Kingdom
- Chef Mickey's in the Contemporary Resort (restaurant)
- Cape May in the Beach Club Resort (restaurant)
- Tusker House in the Animal Kingdom (restaurant)
- Hollywood & Vine in the Hollywood Studios (restaurant)

Donald Duck

- Pete's Silly Sideshow in the Magic Kingdom
- Town Square in the Magic Kingdom in the morning
- Epcot Character Spot
- Mexico Pavilion in Epcot
- Near center stage in front of the Great Movie Ride in the Hollywood Studios
- Near Restaurantosaurus in the Animal Kingdom
- Tusker House in the Animal Kingdom (restaurant)
- Cape May in the Beach Club Resort (restaurant)

- Chef Mickey's in the Contemporary Resort (restaurant)
- Hollywood & Vine in the Hollywood Studios (restaurant)

Daisy Duck

- Pete's Silly Sideshow in the Magic Kingdom
- Town Square in the Magic Kingdom in the morning
- Epcot Character Spot
- In Showcase Plaza in Epcot
- Near center stage in front of the Great Movie Ride in the Hollywood Studios
- Tusker House in the Animal Kingdom (restaurant)
- Chef Mickey's in the Contemporary Resort (restaurant)
- Hollywood & Vine in the Hollywood Studios (restaurant)

Goofy

- Pete's Silly Sideshow in the Magic Kingdom
- Town Square in the Magic Kingdom in the morning
- Main Entrance in Epcot in the morning
- Epcot Character Spot
- Near center stage in front of the Great Movie Ride in the Hollywood Studios
- Dinoland in the Animal Kingdom
- Tusker House in the Animal Kingdom (restaurant)
- Cape May in the Beach Club Resort (restaurant)
- Chef Mickey's in the Contemporary Resort (restaurant)

- Garden Grove in the Swan (restaurant)
- ‘Ohana in the Polynesian Resort (restaurant)
- Hollywood & Vine in the Hollywood Studios (restaurant)

Pluto

- Town Square in the Magic Kingdom in the morning
- Main Entrance in Epcot in the morning
- Epcot Character Spot
- Garden Grill in Epcot (restaurant)
- Near center stage in front of the Great Movie Ride in the Hollywood Studios
- Dinoland in the Animal Kingdom
- Tusker House in the Animal Kingdom (restaurant)
- Chef Mickey’s in the Contemporary Resort (restaurant)
- Garden Grove in the Swan (restaurant)
- ‘Ohana in the Polynesian Resort (restaurant)

Aladdin

- Adventureland near Magic Carpets in the Magic Kingdom
- Morocco Pavilion in Epcot

Alice in Wonderland

- Mad Tea Party in the Magic Kingdom
- United Kingdom Pavilion in Epcot
- 1900 Park Fare in the Grand Floridian Resort (restaurant)

Anastasia and Drisella

- Fantasyland near the Castle in the Magic Kingdom

Anna

- Princess Fairytale Hall in the Magic Kingdom
- Norway Pavilion meet and greet (coming in 2016)

Ariel

- Ariel's Grotto in Fantasyland in the Magic Kingdom
- Cinderella's Royal Table in the Magic Kingdom (restaurant)
- Akershus Royal Banquet Hall in the Norway Pavilion in Epcot (restaurant)

Aurora

- Cinderella's Royal Table in the Magic Kingdom (restaurant)
- Princess Fairytale Hall in the Magic Kingdom
- Town Square in the Magic Kingdom in the morning
- Akershus Royal Banquet Hall in the Norway Pavilion in Epcot (restaurant)

Baymax

- Epcot Character Spot

Belle

- Cinderella's Royal Table in the Magic Kingdom (restaurant)
- France Pavilion in Epcot
- Akershus Royal Banquet Hall in the Norway Pavilion in Epcot (restaurant)

Buzz Lightyear

- Tomorrowland near the Carousel of Progress in the Magic Kingdom

Captain Jack Sparrow

- Adventureland near the Pirates of the Caribbean in the Magic Kingdom

Chewbacca

- Star Wars Launch Bay in the Hollywood Studios

Chip and Dale

- Town Square in the Magic Kingdom in the morning
- Near Epcot Character Spot
- Garden Grill in Epcot (restaurant)
- Near center stage in front of the Great Movie Ride in the Hollywood Studios
- Garden Grove in the Swan (restaurant)

- Rafiki's Planet Watch in the Animal Kingdom

Cinderella

- Cinderella's Royal Table in the Magic Kingdom (restaurant)
- Princess Fairytale Hall in the Magic Kingdom
- Akershus Royal Banquet Hall in the Norway Pavilion (restaurant)
- 1900 Park Fare in the Grand Floridian Resort (restaurant)

Darth Vader

- Star Wars Launch Bay in the Hollywood Studios

Disney Junior Stars

- Animation Courtyard in the Hollywood Studios

Doc McStuffins

- Hollywood & Vine in the Hollywood Studios (restaurant)

Eeyore, Piglet, Pooh Bear, and Tigger

- Crystal Palace in the Magic Kingdom (restaurant)
- Near the Winnie the Pooh attraction in the Magic Kingdom
- United Kingdom Pavilion in Epcot
- Near center stage in front of the Great Movie Ride in the

Hollywood Studios

- Discovery Island in the Animal Kingdom

Elsa

- Princess Fairytale Hall in the Magic Kingdom
- Norway Pavilion meet and greet (coming in 2016)

Fairy Godmother

- In Fantasyland, near the Castle in the Magic Kingdom
- Cinderella's Royal Table in the Magic Kingdom, intermittently (restaurant)
- 1900 Park Fare in the Grand Floridian Resort (restaurant)

Flik

- Discovery Island in the Animal Kingdom

Gaston

- Outside of Gaston's Tavern in the Magic Kingdom

Handy Manny

- Hollywood & Vine in the Hollywood Studios (restaurant)

Incredibles, The

- At the dance party in Tomorrowland in the Magic Kingdom

Jasmine

- Cinderella's Royal Table in the Magic Kingdom (restaurant)
- Morocco Pavilion in Epcot
- Akershus Royal Banquet Hall in the Norway Pavilion in Epcot (restaurant)

Jake of the Neverland Pirates

- Hollywood & Vine in the Hollywood Studios (restaurant)

Jesse

- Near the exit of Splash Mountain in the Magic Kingdom

Lightning McQueen and Mater

- Near Streets of America in the Hollywood Studios

Mad Hatter

- 1900 Park Fare in Grand Floridian Resort (restaurant)

Mary Poppins

- Town Square area in the Magic Kingdom in the morning
- Cinderella's Royal Table in the Magic Kingdom (restaurant)
- United Kingdom Pavilion in Epcot
- Akershus Royal Banquet Hall in the Norway Pavilion in

Epcot (restaurant)

- 1900 Park Fare in the Grand Floridian Resort (restaurant)

Merida

- Fairytale Garden in the Magic Kingdom

Mike Wazowski & Sulley

- Near the Studio Catering Company in the Hollywood Studios

Mulan

- China Pavilion in Epcot
- Akershus Royal Banquet Hall in the Norway Pavilion in Epcot (restaurant)

Peter Pan & Wendy

- Near Peter Pan's Flight in the Magic Kingdom

Phineas and Ferb

- Near Mama Melrose in the Hollywood Studios (restaurant)

Pocahontas

- Character Landing in Discovery Island in the Animal Kingdom

Rafiki

- Rafiki's Planet Watch in the Animal Kingdom

Rapunzel

- Princess Fairytale Hall in the Magic Kingdom

Snow White

- Cinderella's Royal Table in the Magic Kingdom (restaurant)
- Princess Fairytale Hall in the Magic Kingdom
- Front porch of the Town Square Theater in the Magic Kingdom
- Germany Pavilion in Epcot
- Akershus Royal Banquet Hall in the Norway Pavilion in Epcot (restaurant)

Sofia the First

- Hollywood & Vine in the Hollywood Studios (restaurant)

Stitch

- Tomorrowland near the Space Mountain exit in the Magic Kingdom
- 'Ohana in the Polynesian Resort (restaurant)

Tarzan

- Discovery Island in the Animal Kingdom

Tiana

- Liberty Square in the Magic Kingdom

Tinker Bell

- Town Square Theater in the Magic Kingdom

Toy Story Friends

- Pixar Place in the Hollywood Studios

Woody

- Near the Splash Mountain exit in the Magic Kingdom
- Pixar Place near Toy Story Midway Mania in the Hollywood Studios

Chapter 14

Bringing Your Teenager to Walt Disney World

It has been written and thought of so often that Walt Disney World is only for little kids. That is actually NOT true. It is for everyone, even the teenager in your family. This chapter will discuss what your teenager will enjoy about Walt Disney World.

The Magic Kingdom theme park has everything from character meet and greets, slow moving attractions, and rides for the teenager thrill seeker. Usually when anyone sees Mickey Mouse for the first time, they become a child again. Your teenager may fall into this dreamy state. If they do, they can see Mickey in the Town Square Theater or see the Disney princesses in Princess Fairytale Hall.

If your teenager is the thrill seeker type, then the Magic Kingdom has that side too. They can experience the Magic Kingdom mountain range, consisting of: Big Thunder Mountain Railroad, Space Mountain, and Splash Mountain. Big Thunder Mountain will toss them around and have them screaming for more. They will blast off into deep Space on Space Mountain, and they will ride Splash Mountain right into Brer Rabbit's Briar Patch. There is even a stomach clenching drop at the end.

Your teenager thrill seeker can even experience the newest Magic Kingdom attraction, Seven Dwarfs Mine Train. They get to ride in their own mine cart that rocks independently of the others. The dwarfs can even be seen hard at work.

They can get scared in Stitch's Great Escape, visit ghosts in the Haunted Mansion, sing along with their classic Disney favorites in Mickey's PhilharMagic, laugh along with Mike at the Monsters Inc. Laugh Floor, and experience all the United States presidents coming back to life in The Hall of Presidents.

Haunted Mansion gravestone

If they really want be a little kid again, well then the Magic Kingdom has numerous other attractions to tickle their fancy.

Your teenager will need to experience The Twilight Zone Tower of Terror and the Rock 'n' Roller Coaster Starring Aerosmith in Disney's Hollywood Studios. Disney loves to entice your interest with a story, but The Tower of Terror is unlike any story Disney has ever told.

In 1939, guests of the Hollywood Hotel entered an elevator and into a nightmare. They plunged to their demise, and now your teenager can ride in the same elevator!

The Rock 'n' Roller Coaster Starring Aerosmith will get your teenager screaming. The ride begins motionless and then rockets to 60mph in 2.8 seconds! Make sure to ask a Disney cast member to sit in the front seat if a real rush is needed!

The Hollywood Studios is even home to such movies as Star Wars and Indiana Jones. Your teenager will see C-3PO, R2D2, and many other Star Wars characters as they ride in a transport to numerous destinations.

Over at the Indiana Jones Epic Stunt Spectacular, the cast shows the audience how the stunts from the movies actually occur. Your teenager could even be picked to be an extra during the show.

If your energetic teenager was a huge Toy Story fan growing up, they can relive their childhood experience with Woody, Buzz, and the gang on the attraction Toy Story Midway Mania! This attraction takes you on a 4D adventure to play carnival style games. The ride system keeps track of points and your teenager could record the high score for the day.

Epcot is not just a World's Fair. It contains thrill rides, fascinating attractions, and countries from all over the world. The thrill side of the park are the attractions: Mission: Space, Soarin, Sum of All Thrills, and Test Track. Mission: Space will rocket your teenager to Mars. Depending on their motion sickness vulnerability, they do have the chance of getting sick if they choose the orange team.

Soarin may not completely be a thrill attraction, however, it is a must see experience for everyone. All of your senses are enticed as you fly over different areas of California.

Your teenager will just be yelling, "Yes, Yes!" as they experience Test Track. They will be able to ride in a test vehicle that seats six, and travel 65 mph in an open air car. They even are able to design a vehicle and visit a showroom that has the newest cars for the upcoming year.

The Sum of All Thrills is a little known attraction that I have written about earlier in this book. Your teenager can use their years of schooling in Math and Science and design their own thrill ride. When it is good to go, they take a seat in a simulator and experience the ride they just designed.

World Showcase is a section of Epcot that everyone should take in. Eleven countries are represented displaying their culture for all to see. The cast members in all of these countries are from the country they represent. You teenager can taste outstanding food and visually be fascinated by the architecture of the host country.

Disney's Animal Kingdom theme park is as much fun as a

teenager sending out a tweet to all of their followers. It is the home of attractions with distinguishing names such as: Expedition Everest, Dinosaur, Primeval Whirl, and Kali River Rapids. Those names just scream, “Exhilarating!”

Expedition Everest is one of the best attractions in Walt Disney World. Your teenager will ride in a train that the Yeti (abominable snowman) will attack. The train goes forward and backwards in complete darkness, and even goes down some mind rushing drops.

In Dinoland U.S.A., they will come face to face with the creatures that ruled the Earth 65 million years ago. The Dinosaur attraction is very dark as the creatures attack the timer rover. Your teenager can ride it again and again!

Dinosaur!

Primeval Whirl has enough quick drops, twists, and turns

for everyone. It is an outdoor single car coaster that is just steps away from Dinosaur.

Kali River Rapids will almost definitely get your teenager soaked. However, depending on the weather, that may be just up their alley. The large raft goes through high speed rapids as water splashes and sprays from all directions.

The show "Festival of the Lion King" is a Broadway style production that your teenager initially may think is only for little kids. But, before it is over, they will be singing along with their favorite "Lion King" songs.

Kilimanjaro Safaris is like actually going on an African Safari, without traveling all the way to Africa. The tour vehicle will drive in the open savannah while elephants, rhinos, and numerous other animals may come right up to the vehicle.

Elephant from Kilimanjaro Safaris

The Disney Springs area is a section of Walt Disney World that your teenager may also enjoy. They can shop until they drop, eat in restaurants like T-Rex and Fulton's Crab House, grab some ice cream, or just wander around and explore the area.

There are numerous restaurants your teenage will thoroughly enjoy. Beaches and Cream, located in Disney's Beach Club Resort, is an old fashioned diner that specializes in burgers, hot dogs, fries, and sundaes. Along with Beaches and Cream is Cape May in the Beach Club. Cape May serves a clam bake buffet and many other choices for dinner.

The ESPN Club is a great place to eat a meal and have your teenager watch their favorite sports team on the big screen. Boma is another Walt Disney World resort restaurant your teenager may enjoy. They can feast on African food at this enormous buffet in Disney's Animal Kingdom Lodge.

The theme parks all have restaurants that will make anyone's mouth water. Check out Be Our Guest restaurant and Tony's Town Square in the Magic Kingdom. In the Hollywood Studios your teenager may enjoy 50s Prime Time Café, Mama Melrose, and the Sci-Fi restaurant.

In Epcot your teenager can dine on all types of foods from various cultures. Some of those restaurants are: Le Cellier, Nine Dragons, Rose and Crown, Teppan Edo, Tutto Italia, and Via Napoli.

There are many other restaurants in Walt Disney World

you and your teenager may want to experience. Please refer back to chapter five on dining recommendations for other restaurants and detailed descriptions of the ones listed in this chapter.

Your teenager will be astounded by the pools in the various Walt Disney World resorts. The value resorts, which are the All Star Sports, All Star Movies, All Star Music, Pop Century, and Art of Animation, all have enormous pools, but they do not have slides.

The pools in the moderate and deluxe resorts all have specific themes and do have fabulous slides. Disney's Beach Club Resort pool has a sandy bottom and even a lazy river.

If you are staying on Walt Disney World property, your teenager can take advantage of the extra magic hours. As described earlier in the book, extra magic hours is when a theme park will open an hour early or a theme park will stay open two or three extra hours after the park has closed. This is for Walt Disney World resort guests only.

If your teenager is an early riser, they can get going right away and enjoy the attractions. However, my gut tells me your child enjoys to sleep in during their teen years. If this is the case, they can use the extra magic hours at night. Just refer to the guide in your resort for the theme park that is staying open late that day. Your teenager will be able to enjoy that theme park until late at night and, if you choose, you can let them experience this without you.

Walt Disney World is filled with security precautions everywhere. There are cameras watching everyone's move so you have nothing to worry about. When they are ready to return to the resort, the Walt Disney World transportation will pick them up and drop them off. The Disney buses operate every 20 minutes. The boats and monorails are constantly running until everyone is out of the theme parks.

Chapter 15

Top 10 Mistakes People Make in Walt Disney World

1) They do not make dining reservations 180 days in advance.

There are numerous fabulous restaurants in Walt Disney World, and the most popular restaurants book up very quickly. The restaurants that book up typically 180 days in advance are: Be Our Guest Restaurant in the Magic Kingdom, Cinderella's Royal Table in the Magic Kingdom, Chef Mickey's in Disney's Contemporary Resort, Akershus in Epcot, and the Hoop Dee Doo Revue in Disney's Fort Wilderness.

If you want to dine in one of these fabulous restaurants then make a note on your calendar to make your dining reservation 180 days in advance.

Even if a restaurant that you want to dine in is not listed above, I would still call about 180 days in advance or so to be confident you get a suitable time. I am sure no one in your family wants to eat dinner at 9pm at the Crystal Palace in the Magic Kingdom, for example.

If you do encounter a problem because you waited too long, you could attempt to get a dining reservation for lunch. Lunch is not as busy and may get you out of a jam, especially if you know the family is going to be very upset.

Please do not assume you will be able to walk up to a restaurant and get on a waiting list. The host or hostess will either tell you it is a very long wait for a table or they may say the dreaded words that will turn your smile into a frown, "We are completely booked tonight."

2) Families believe they will experience everything and go from morning until night.

I have personal experience with this concept. The first few times I went to Walt Disney World with only my wife. The children were only a sparkle in our eye. We were so excited, and we wanted to experience everything in a week.

It is just not possible! We got up every day at 7am. I would jump in the shower and get dressed. As my wife was getting ready, I ran to the food court in Disney's All Star Sports Resort and grabbed a muffin for each of us, coffee, and orange juice.

I flew back to the room like Superman going to rescue Lois Lane! We would scarf down our muffins and off we would go to the bus stop in front of the resort by 8am.

We would get to the theme park of our choice 30 minutes before it opened. We went from attraction to attraction, having the time of our lives, grab a quick lunch, go and experience more excitement, and eat dinner around 9pm.

We would get back to our resort by about 11pm and be exhausted, but we were ready for more the next day.

We tried this schedule for 4 straight days until we went on

the Human Heart ride in Epcot. This attraction is no longer there, but it was a simulator, and it bounced you around like a small child being in a bouncy house with a person who only shops at the Big and Tall stores. We were so exhausted that the ride did us in, and our bodies said, "That is enough!" My wife almost became ill and said, "Can we please go back and rest in the resort?"

My mind was saying, "There is so much to see here," but I knew the right choice to make. It was time for a break. We felt like a dog that was yelled at by his owner. We put our heads down and left the park.

You could go to Walt Disney World every day for 3 to 4 weeks straight and still not experience everything the resort complex has to offer. It is not a restful vacation, but don't make your family sick like I almost did to my wife.

3) Visitors wait in a long line to take a picture with a character.

There are ways to avoid waiting in a huge line for Mickey, Minnie, or a princess, just to name a few characters. The easiest way is to make a dining reservation with the character your family wants to visit. This way there will be no waiting in that long line.

Please refer back to the chapter on the location of your favorite character to check the dining location you will find a specific character.

If you need to see the Frozen characters Anna and Elsa, then you need to make your FastPass+ selection for Princess Fairytale Hall in the Magic Kingdom 60 days in advance. You should do this a little after midnight. As of January 2016, Anna and Elsa are not in any dining location.

There are some characters who do not appear in any restaurant. Two examples would be Woody and Buzz from Toy Story. You will have to wait in line to get a picture with them and an autograph.

4) Vacationers think that visiting Epcot is a waste of time.

Spaceship Earth in the distance

The people who make this type of statement have not truly explored and experienced the true beauty and majestic character that Epcot contains.

Mission: Space, Soarin, Spaceship Earth, and Test Track are attractions that will entice your mind and two will definitely push your body to the limits as you fly to Mars or go 65mph!

Yes there is an educational side to Epcot, but it is still exciting to visit what Walt Disney himself imagined for Epcot. Ellen's Energy Adventure is a fun way to learn about energy. Living with the Land takes you on a boat ride to experience how the Earth is used by the people. The Seas with Nemo and Friends contains one of the largest aquariums on the planet. You will view ocean fish, sharks, and dolphins.

You can even visit the characters in Epcot at the Character Spot. One character your child may want to see is Crush from Finding Nemo. You can take your child to Turtle Talk with Crush, listen to his funny jokes and he may even speak directly to your child.

The eleven countries in World Showcase are truly spectacular. The cast members in each country are from that home country. You can taste the particular country's food in one of their snack shops or restaurants. A few of them even have attractions or films about the home country. Epcot is something you will not want to miss!

5) WDW guests think that Animal Kingdom is a zoo!

This statement could not be more false. There is a section of Animal Kingdom that contains live animals, but the animals are not in cages. While you go on two different walking trails you will see animals in their natural habitat, walking free, and exploring their environment.

You can experience a real African Safari while riding on Kilimanjaro Safaris. Your jeep vehicle, which is driven by a cast member, will take you into the African savannah where all the animals roam freely and an animal may even walk right up to the jeep.

Elephants in Kilimanjaro Safaris

Animal Kingdom does have a section for the thrill seeker in your family. The attractions include: Dinosaur, Expedition Everest, Kali River Rapids, and Primeval Whirl.

Animal Kingdom even houses a Broadway style show titled Festival of the Lion King.

You will want to check out the Tusker House to have a meal with Donald and Friends. The food is delicious, and the company will make you smile for the rest of the day. Make sure you do not miss Animal Kingdom!

6) Families do not make dining reservations at different Walt Disney World resort restaurants.

Some people do not realize or do not want to bother making dining reservations in a few of the Walt Disney World resorts. This, in my opinion, is a huge mistake.

There are so many spectacular restaurants in the resorts. If you travel on the monorail loop you can dine with Mickey and friends at Chef Mickey's and the California Grille in Disney's Contemporary Resort is spectacular. You can meet Cinderella and Prince Charming at 1900 Park Fare in Disney's Grand Floridian Resort. Mickey and friends are over at 'Ohana in Disney's Polynesian Resort too!

Disney's Beach Club resort has two distinctly different restaurants, and both are superb. Cape May is a character meal for breakfast and a clam bake buffet for dinner. Beaches and

Cream is an old fashioned establishment serving burgers, hot dogs, fries, and mouthwatering sundaes.

Boma is a family favorite located in Disney's Animal Kingdom Lodge. The Hoop Dee Doo Musical Revue is a dinner show located in Disney's Fort Wilderness. These are just a few of the resort restaurants you will want to visit while in WDW. If you take some time away from the theme parks you will not turn into a pumpkin.

7) The general public visits a theme park that has morning extra magic hours, but do not arrive when the park opens.

You may be asking yourself, why is it so important to get to the theme park before it opens when there is an extra hour in the morning? The reason is simply this: a majority of people staying in a WDW resort will visit that early morning park. If you get there late you will always be behind. The early morning risers will maximize their time in the park and ride the most popular attractions multiple times by using the standby line.

This does not mean you should always visit the theme park that opens early. There have been many visits where I have avoided the early theme park like the plague. Always check the park hours in advance to see which park opens early in the morning. Either arrive before the park opens, or do not visit there at all.

The same philosophy goes for people not staying in a

WDW resort. Check the theme park hours and do not visit a theme park if it has morning extra magic hours. When you make this wise decision your family will look at you later as the Einstein of the family.

8) People make FastPass+ selections for attractions that typically have very short wait times.

This is a common mistake. The attractions that fall into this category are listed here. I have detailed in previous chapters the attractions I would recommend obtaining a FastPass+ and the ones that will have a very short wait.

In the Magic Kingdom you do not need a FastPass+ for certain attractions which include but are not limited to: Mickey's PhilharMagic, Mad Tea Party, Magic Carpets of Aladdin, Monster's Inc. Laugh Floor, Wishes, and the day or nighttime parades.

In Epcot you do not need a FastPass+ for: Illuminations, Journey into Imagination with Figment, and Living with the Land.

Over in the Hollywood Studios, do not waste a FastPass+ on Fantasmic. It is an amazing show, but you can use the Fantasmic dining package to get a good seat.

Muppet Vision 3D and Voyage of the Little Mermaid are two other attractions where you can get away without having to obtain a FastPass+.

In the Animal Kingdom, the three attractions where a FastPass+ is not necessary are: Flights of Wonder, It's Tough to be a Bug, and Festival of the Lion King. I do recommend that you arrive approximately 25 minutes before Festival of the Lion King begins to assure entrance into that show.

9) Visitors to WDW use a FastPass+ for Fantasmic.

Fantasmic is one of the must see shows in Walt Disney World. However, do not use a FastPass+ selection for it. You can instead make a reservation for the Fantasmic Dining Package. I have described this previously, but I will mention it again.

You can call Disney dining at (407) WDW-DINE. You reserve the Fantasmic Dining Package by either dining at Hollywood & Vine, Mama Melrose, or the Hollywood Brown Derby. It is extremely important that you tell the dining representative that you want the Fantasmic Dining Package and not just a normal dining reservation. By making this reservation you are guaranteed good seats for Fantasmic.

If you choose Fantasmic as one of your FastPass+ selections, then you will not be able to get a 4th FastPass+ after you have used your initial three selections. The reason for this is that Fantasmic is not performed until an hour or so before the Hollywood Studios closes. When the show ends, the park will either be closing or no FastPass+ times will be available.

10) Guests rent a car when they are staying in a WDW resort.

Walt Disney World Resort has an enormous fleet of transportation to shuttle you around the property. You will be taken to all of the theme parks, Disney Springs, Blizzard Beach, Typhon Lagoon, and back to your resort.

The buses do run every 20 minutes or so. Unless you just cannot wait a few extra minutes, you have no reason to rent a car. You will even save a few hundred dollars if you are on a budget.

Chapter 16

One Day Theme Park Itineraries

For years people have asked me, "What system do you follow to maximize your time in the theme parks?" There are numerous answers to that question. However, I have decided to put some ideas down on paper and show the world a possible park itinerary for each theme park in WDW. I will break down each theme park by age group and certain very specific criteria that must be followed to the "letter" or the itinerary will not work.

One criteria is you must arrive 30 minutes before a theme park opens. I don't mean getting out of your car or exiting the bus 30 minutes before the park opens. You will need to be in line with a big smile on your face 30 minutes ahead of time.

The other criteria is making the three FastPass+ selections 60 days in advance a few minutes after midnight so you are able to obtain the selections I will suggest along with times. This is not completely fool proof, but you will be ahead of the crowds all day long!

Magic Kingdom Itinerary ages 1-7

- FastPass+ selections (Seven Dwarfs Mine Train 9:30-10:30am, The Many Adventures of Winnie the Pooh 10:30-11:30am, Enchanted Tales with Belle 11:30am-12:30pm)

1. Enter the Magic Kingdom at 9am or when it opens.
2. Go to Princess FairyTale Hall

3. Visit The Barnstormer
4. Use your FastPass+ for the Seven Dwarfs Mine Train 9:30-10:30am
5. Ride Peter Pan's Flight
6. Ride Under the Sea – Journey of the Little Mermaid
7. Use your FastPass+ for The Many Adventures of Winnie the Pooh 10:30-11:30am
8. Ariel's Grotto
9. Dumbo
10. Use your FastPass+ for Enchanted Tales with Belle 11:30am-12:30pm
11. Visit the FastPass+ kiosk near Mickey's PhilharMagic and make a selection for Buzz Lightyear Space Ranger Spin
12. Eat lunch at Be Our Guest (call 407-WDW-DINE 180 days in advance for a reservation at 1pm)
13. Tomorrowland Speedway
14. Mad Tea Party
15. Carousel of Progress
16. Tomorrowland Transit Authority PeopleMover
17. Monster's Inc. Laugh Floor
18. Use your FastPass+ for Buzz Lightyear Space Ranger Spin
19. Visit the FastPass+ kiosk near Stitch's Great Escape and make a selection for the Jungle Cruise

20. Pirates of the Caribbean
21. The Magic Carpets of Aladdin
22. Eat dinner at Crystal Palace (call 407-WDW-DINE 180 days in advance for a reservation)
23. Use your FastPass+ for Jungle Cruise
24. Haunted Mansion
25. It's a small world
26. See the Main Street Electrical Parade
27. Watch Wishes

These attractions can fit into your schedule at any time: Sorcerers of the Magic Kingdom, Swiss Family Tree House, A Pirate's Adventure, Pirates League, Walt Disney World Railroad, Tom Sawyer Island, Country Bear Jamboree, Mickey's PhilharMagic, Carrousel, Liberty Square Riverboat, Disney Festival of Fantasy Parade (usually at 3pm), and Casey Jr. Splash 'N' Soak Station.

Magic Kingdom Itinerary ages 8-12

- FastPass+ selections (Big Thunder Mountain Railroad 9:30-10:30am, Seven Dwarfs Mine Train 10:30-11:30am, Space Mountain 11:30am-12:30pm)

1. Enter the Magic Kingdom at 9am or when it opens
2. Visit Princess Fairytale Hall, if needed
3. Ride Splash Mountain (maybe twice)

Splash Mountain

4. Ride Big Thunder Mountain
5. Use your FastPass+ for Big Thunder Mountain Railroad 9:30-10:30am
6. Ride the Haunted Mansion
7. Use your FastPass+ for the Seven Dwarfs Mine Train 10:30-11:30am
8. The Many Adventures of Winnie the Pooh
9. Tomorrowland Speedway
10. Use your FastPass+ for Space Mountain 11:30am-12:30pm
11. Visit the FastPass+ kiosk near Stitch's Great Escape and make a FastPass+ selection for Peter Pan's Flight
12. Eat Lunch at the Starlight Café

13. Monster's Inc. Laugh Floor
14. Stitch's Great Escape
15. Tomorrowland Transit Authority PeopleMover
16. Carousel of Progress
17. Mad Tea Party
18. Use your FastPass+ for Peter Pan's Flight
19. Visit the FastPass+ kiosk next to Mickey's PhilharMagic and make a FastPass+ selection for Enchanted Tales with Belle
20. It's a small world
21. Eat dinner in Tony's Town Square or Crystal Palace if you make a dining reservation in advance
22. Under the Sea – Journey of the Little Mermaid
23. Dumbo the Flying Elephant
24. Ariel's Grotto
25. Use your FastPass+ for Enchanted Tales with Belle
26. Main Street Electrical Parade
27. Wishes
28. The Magic Carpets of Aladdin
29. Pirates of the Caribbean
30. Jungle Cruise
31. Buzz Lightyear's Space Ranger Spin

These attractions can fit into your schedule at any time: Mickey's PhilharMagic, Carrousel, Casey Jr. Splash 'N' Soak Station, Liberty Square Riverboat, Hall of Presidents, Disney

Festival of Fantasy Parade (usually at 3pm), A Pirate's Adventure, Pirates League, and the Walt Disney World Railroad.

Magic Kingdom Itinerary ages 13-adults

- FastPass+ selections (Big Thunder Mountain Railroad 9:30-10:30am, Seven Dwarfs Mine Train 10:30-11:30am, Space Mountain 11:30am-12:30pm)

1. Enter the Magic Kingdom at 9am or when it opens
2. Ride Splash Mountain (possibly twice)
3. Use your FastPass+ for Big Thunder Mountain Railroad 9:30-10:30am
4. Ride the Pirates of the Caribbean
5. Jungle Cruise
6. Use your FastPass+ for the Seven Dwarfs Mine Train 10:30-11:30am
7. Buzz Lightyear's Space Ranger Spin
8. Monster's Inc. Laugh Floor
9. Use your FastPass+ for Space Mountain 11:30am-12:30pm
10. Visit the FastPass+ kiosk next to Stitch's Great Escape and obtain a FastPass+ for the Haunted Mansion or a desired attraction
11. Eat lunch
12. Visit Stitch's Great Escape
13. Carousel of Progress

14. Tomorrowland Transit Authority PeopleMover
15. Mad Tea Party
16. Under the Sea – Journey of the Little Mermaid
17. It's a small world
18. Use your FastPass+ for the Haunted Mansion
19. Visit the Hall of Presidents
20. Visit the FastPass+ kiosk between the Diamond Horseshoe and the Frontier Trading Post and obtain a FastPass+ for a desired attraction.
21. Eat dinner
22. Ride the attractions that you want to experience again
23. Main Street Electrical Parade
24. Use your FastPass+ for your desired attraction
25. Peter Pan's Flight
26. Wishes

These attractions can fit into your schedule at any time: Mickey's PhilharMagic, Disney Festival of Fantasy Parade (usually at 3pm), Walt Disney World Railroad, and the Liberty Square Riverboat.

Epcot Itinerary for ages 1-7

- FastPass+ selections (Spaceship Earth 9:30-10:30am, Soarin 10:30-11:30am, The Seas with Nemo & Friends 11:30am-12:30pm)

1. Enter Epcot at 9am or when it opens

2. Ride Test Track
3. Use your FastPass+ for Spaceship Earth 9:30-10:30am
4. The Circle of Life
5. Ride Living with the Land
6. Use your FastPass+ for Soarin 10:30-11:30am
7. Disney & Pixar Short Film Festival
8. Use your FastPass+ for the Seas with Nemo & Friends 11:30am-12:30pm
9. Explore the Seas Pavilion
10. Visit the FastPass+ kiosk near the Electric Umbrella and get a FastPass+ for Turtle Talk with Crush
11. Eat lunch at the Electric Umbrella
12. Visit Ellen's Energy Adventure
13. Explore the Innoventions buildings
14. Use your FastPass+ for Turtle Talk with Crush
15. Visit the 11 countries
16. Eat dinner in a country (make a dinner reservation 180 days in advance)
17. Illuminations

These attractions can fit into your schedule at any time: Journey into Imagination with Figment, Agent P's World Showcase Adventure, Epcot Character Spot, and try to obtain a 5th or 6th FastPass+.

Epcot Itinerary for ages 8-12

- FastPass+ selections (Spaceship Earth 9:30-10:30am, Soarin 10:30-11:30am, Disney & Pixar Short Film Festival 11:30am-12:30pm)

1. Enter Epcot at 9am or when it opens
2. Ride Test Track
3. The Sum of All Thrills
4. Use your FastPass+ for Spaceship Earth 9:30-10:30am
5. The Circle of Life
6. Living with the Land
7. Use the FastPass+ for Soarin 10:30-11:30am
8. Mission: Space
9. Use your FastPass+ for Disney & Pixar Short Film Festival 11:30am-12:30pm
10. Visit the FastPass+ kiosk near the Electric Umbrella and get a FastPass+ for The Seas with Nemo & Friends
11. Eat lunch at the Electric Umbrella
12. Ellen's Energy Adventure
13. Explore the Innoventions buildings
14. Use the FastPass+ for The Seas with Nemo & Friends
15. Explore the Seas Pavilion
16. Turtle Talk with Crush
17. Visit the 11 countries
18. Eat dinner in a country (make a dinner reservation 180 days in advance)

19. Illuminations

Epcot Itinerary for ages 13-adult

- FastPass+ selections (Spaceship Earth 9:30-10:30am, Soarin 10:30-11:30am, Disney & Pixar Short Film Festival 11:30am-12:30pm)

1. Enter Epcot at 9am or when it opens
2. Ride Test Track
3. The Sum of All Thrills
4. Use the FastPass+ for Spaceship Earth 9:30-10:30am
5. Living with the Land
6. Use the FastPass+ for Soarin 10:30-11:30am
7. Mission: Space
8. Explore the Innoventions buildings
9. Use the FastPass+ for Disney & Pixar Short Film Festival 11:30am-12:30pm
10. Visit the FastPass+ kiosk near the Electric Umbrella and make a 4th FastPass+ for a desired attraction
11. Eat lunch at the Electric Umbrella
12. Ellen's Energy Adventure
13. Explore the Seas Pavilion
14. Visit the 11 countries
15. Use your 4th FastPass+
16. Eat dinner in a country (make a dinner reservation 180 days in advance)

17. Illuminations

These attractions can fit into your schedule at any time: Epcot Character Spot, the Circle of Life, and try to obtain a 5th or 6th FastPass+.

Disney's Hollywood Studios Itinerary for ages 1-7

- FastPass+ selections (Toy Story Midway Mania 9:30-10:30am, Great Movie Ride 10:30-11:30am, Beauty and the Beast 11:30am-12:30pm (possible 12noon show)

1. Enter the Studios at 9am or when it opens
2. Sign up your child for the Jedi Training Academy
3. Use child swap or everyone ride the Tower of Terror
4. Use your FastPass+ for Toy Story Midway Mania 9:30-10:30am
5. Visit the Star Wars Launch Bay
6. Use your FastPass+ for The Great Movie Ride 10:30-11:30am
7. Experience Voyage of the Little Mermaid
8. Use your FastPass+ for Beauty and the Beast 11:30am-12:30pm (possible 12noon show)
9. Visit the FastPass+ kiosk in front of the Tower of Terror and obtain a FastPass+ for Star Tours
10. Eat Lunch at Catalina Eddie's or Rosie's All-American Café
11. See Disney-Junior-Live on Stage (possible 1:30pm show)
12. Muppet Vision 3D

13. Jedi Training show (possible 3:30ish show)
14. Use your FastPass+ for Star Tours
15. Visit the FastPass+ kiosk to the right of Muppet Vision 3D and obtain a FastPass+ for Fantasmic if you did not make a reservation for the Fantasmic dining package or for another desired attraction
16. For the First Time in Forever: A Frozen Sing-Along Celebration
17. Indiana Jones Epic Stunt Spectacular
18. Eat dinner in one of the many dining locations in the Studios (call 180 days in advance)
19. See Fantasmic!

These attractions can fit into your schedule at any time: Walt Disney: One Man's Dream, Citizens of Hollywood, Lights, Motors, Action Extreme Stunt Show (closing April 2016), and Honey I Shrunk the Kids Movie Set Adventure (closing April 2016).

Disney's Hollywood Studios Itinerary for ages 8-12

- FastPass+ selections (Tower of Terror 10:00-11:00am, Toy Story Midway Mania 11:00am-12:00pm, Star Tours 12:00-1:00pm)

1. Enter the Studios at 9am or when it opens
2. Sign up your child for the Jedi Training Academy
3. Ride the Rock 'n' Roller Coaster or use child swap

4. Go through the standby line for the Tower of Terror
5. Use your FastPass+ for the Tower of Terror 10:00-11:00am
6. Visit the Voyage of the Little Mermaid
7. Use your FastPass+ for Toy Story Midway Mania 11:00am-12:00pm
8. Visit the Star Wars Launch Bay
9. Use your FastPass+ for Star Tours 12:00-1:00pm
10. Visit the FastPass+ kiosk next to Muppet Vision 3D and obtain a FastPass+ for The Great Movie Ride
11. Eat lunch in the Backlot Express
12. Visit Muppet Vision 3D
13. For the First Time in Forever: A Frozen Sing-Along Celebration (possible 2pm show)
14. Visit the Indiana Jones Epic Stunt Spectacular (possible 3pm show)
15. Jedi Training show (possible 4ish show)
16. Use your FastPass+ for the Great Movie Ride
17. Visit the FastPass+ kiosk near Toy Story Midway Mania and obtain a FastPass+ for Fantasmic if you did not make a reservation for the Fantasmic dining package or for another desired attraction
18. See Beauty and the Beast-Live on Stage (possible 5pm show)
19. Eat dinner in one of the many dining locations in the

Studios (call 180 days in advance)

20. See Fantasmic!

These attractions can fit into your schedule at any time: Walt Disney: One Man's Dream, Citizens of Hollywood, Lights, Motors, Action Extreme Stunt Show (closing April 2016), and Honey I Shrunk the Kids Movie Set Adventure (closing April 2016).

Disney's Hollywood Studios Itinerary for ages 13-adult

- FastPass+ selections (Tower of Terror 10:00-11:00am, Toy Story Midway Mania 11:00am-12:00pm, Star Tours 12:00-1:00pm)

1. Enter the Studios at 9am or when it opens
2. Ride the Rock 'n' Roller Coaster
3. Go through the standby line for the Tower of Terror
4. Use your FastPass+ for the Tower of Terror 10:00-11:00am
5. Visit the Star Wars Launch Bay
6. Use your FastPass+ for Toy Story Midway Mania 11:00am-12:00pm
7. Experience the Voyage of the Little Mermaid
8. Use your FastPass+ for Star Tours 12:00-1:00pm
9. Visit the FastPass+ kiosk next to Muppet Vision 3D and obtain a 4th FastPass+ for The Great Movie Ride
10. Eat lunch in the Backlot Express

11. See Muppet Vision 3D
12. Experience Indiana Jones Epic Stunt Spectacular (possible 2:00ish show)
13. See Beauty and the Beast-Live on Stage (possible 3:00ish show)
14. Use your FastPass+ for The Great Movie Ride
15. Visit the FastPass+ kiosk near Toy Story Midway Mania and obtain a FastPass+ for Fantasmic if you did not make a reservation for the Fantasmic dining package or for another desired attraction
16. Check your mydisneyexperience app to see which attraction has a wait time of 25 minutes or less and visit that attraction
17. Eat dinner in one of the many dining locations in the Studios (call 180 days in advance)
18. See Fantasmic

These attractions can fit into your schedule at any time: Walt Disney: One Man's Dream, Citizens of Hollywood; and Lights, Motors, and Action Extreme Stunt Show (closing April 2016).

Disney's Animal Kingdom Itinerary for ages 1-7

- FastPass+ selections (Kilimanjaro Safaris 9:30-10:30am, Festival of the Lion King 10:30-11:30am (possible 11am show), and Finding Nemo-The Musical 11:30am-12:30pm

(possible 12pm show)

1. Enter the Animal Kingdom at 9am or when it opens
2. Visit the Adventurers Outpost
3. Use your FastPass+ selection for Kilimanjaro Safaris 9:30-10:30am
4. Visit the Pangani Forest Exploration Trail
5. Use your FastPass+ for Festival of the Lion King 10:30-11:30am (possible 11am show)
6. Use your FastPass+ for Finding Nemo-The Musical 11:30am-12:30pm (possible 12pm show)
7. Eat lunch in Restaurantosaurus
8. Visit TriceraTop Spin
9. Play a few carnival games in Dinoland, U.S.A. (Fossil Fun Games)
10. Experience Dinosaur if your child can handle dark experiences and if they are at least 40"
11. Visit the FastPass+ kiosk next to Kali River Rapids and obtain a 4th FastPass+ for a desired attraction
12. Experience Kali River Rapids <u>(you will get soaked)</u>
13. See Flights of Wonder (possible 3:45 show)
14. Maharajah Jungle Trek
15. It's Tough to be a Bug
16. Use your 4th FastPass+
17. Eat dinner in the Tusker House (Make a reservation 180 days in advance)

These attractions can fit into your schedule at any time: Habitat Habit, Conservation Station, Affection Section, Wilderness Explorers, Discovery Island Trails, and The Boneyard.

<u>**Disney's Animal Kingdom Itinerary for ages 8-adult**</u>

- FastPass+ selections (Expedition Everest 9:30-10:30am, Dinosaur 10:30-11:30am, Kilimanjaro Safaris 12:00-1:00pm)

1. Enter Disney's Animal Kingdom at 9am or when it opens
2. Go in the standby line for Expedition Everest
3. Use your FastPass+ for Expedition Everest 9:30-10:30am
4. Ride Kali River Rapids <u>(you will get soaked)</u>
5. Maharajah Jungle Trek
6. Use your FastPass+ for Dinosaur 10:30-11:30am
7. Visit Primeval Whirl
8. The Boneyard (If anyone wants to go on a playground)
9. Use your FastPass+ for Kilimanjaro Safaris 12:00-1:00pm
10. Visit the FastPass+ kiosk near the Harambe Market and obtain a FastPass+ for Finding Nemo-The Musical (4:00ish show) or Flights of Wonder (3:45ish show)
11. Eat lunch in the Harambe Market
12. Festival of the Lion King (possible 2:00ish show)
13. Visit Pangani Forest Exploration Trail
14. Use the FastPass+ for Finding Nemo or Flights of Wonder
15. It's Tough to be a Bug

16. Eat dinner in the Tusker House Restaurant (make a dining reservation 180 days in advance – Mickey and Minnie are at the Tusker House so you do not have to visit the Adventurers Outpost.)

These attractions can fit into your schedule at any time: Habitat Habit, Conservation Station, Affection Section, Wilderness Explorers, Discovery Island Trails, and Fossil Fun Games.

Walt Disney World is a magical place where family memories can be made that will last a lifetime. My daughter Megan, and my son Merino, still count down the days until our next trip to visit the "Mouse." I hope my book was just the right size for you to read because I know very well that busy families do not have time to sit down, let alone read a six hundred page book to go on a vacation. Follow all my tips that I have included, and you will not be disappointed. The tips will help you and your busy family plan a wonderful trip and guide you through the theme parks stress free.

Please make sure you visit my website www.mousevacationplanning.com as well. I hope you have an incredible time and love Walt Disney World as much as my family and I do!

"Partners" statue of Walt Disney and Mickey Mouse

Walt Disney World Phone Numbers

Bibbidi Bobbidi Boutique 407-WDW-7895

Car Care Center 407-824-3470

Disney's Magical Express 866-599-0951

Grand Floridian Spa 407-WDW-SPAS

Harmony Barber Shop 407-WDW-PLAY

Pirates League 407-WDW-CREW

Saratoga Springs Spa 407-WDW-SPAS

T-Rex Restaurant 407-828-8739

Walt Disney World Dining 407-WDW-DINE

Walt Disney World Golf 407-WDW-GOLF

Walt Disney World Information 407-824-2222

Walt Disney World Merchandise 877-560-6477

Walt Disney World Travel 407-WDISNEY

Resort Phone Numbers

All Star Movies Resort 407-939-7000

All Star Music 407-939-6000

All Star Sports 407-939-5000

Animal Kingdom Lodge 407-938-3000

Animal Kingdom Villas 407-938-7400

Art of Animation 407-938-7000

Bay Lake Tower 407-824-1000

Beach Club 407-934-8000

Beach Club Villas 407-934-2175

Boardwalk Inn and Villas 407-939-5100

Caribbean Beach 407-934-3400

Contemporary 407-824-1000

Coronado Springs 407-939-1000

Fort Wilderness 407-824-2900

Grand Floridian and Villas 407-824-3000

Old Key West 407-827-7700

Polynesian 407-824-2000

Pop Century 407-938-4000

Port Orleans French Quarter 407-934-5000

Port Orleans Riverside 407-934-6000

Saratoga Springs and Treehouse Villas 407-827-1100

Shades of Green 407-824-3600

Walt Disney World Dolphin 407-934-4000

Walt Disney World Swan 407-934-3000

Wilderness Lodge 407-824-3200

Wilderness Lodge Villas 407-938-4300

Yacht Club 407-934-7000

32214499R00179

Made in the USA
Middletown, DE
26 May 2016